KV-376-304

THE MY WORD! STORIES

Derived from the popular radio panel game in which Frank Muir and Denis Norden are each given a well-known saying and have to work it into an amusing fictional story.

Here in a single paperback volume, the full texts of two best-sellers: *You Can't Have Your Kayak and Heat It* and *Upon My Word!*

Frank Muir & Denis Norden

THE
MY WORD!
STORIES

from the panel game devised by
Edward J. Mason & Tony Shryane

Combining in one volume the complete texts of
You Can't Have Your Kayak and Heat It
and *Upon My Word!*

Methuen Paperbacks
Eyre Methuen

The MY WORD! Stories (this combined paperback edition
of *You Can't Have Your Kayak and Heat It* and *Upon My Word!*)
first published 1976
by Eyre Methuen Ltd, 11 New Fetter Lane, London EC4P 4EE
Reprinted 1976

ISBN 0 413 34750 8 (Methuen Paperback)

You Can't Have Your Kayak and Heat It first published 1973
Upon My Word! first published 1974 by Eyre Methuen Ltd
Copyright © 1973, 1974, 1976 by Frank Muir and Denis Norden

Printed in Great Britain
by Hazell Watson & Viney Ltd, Aylesbury, Bucks

CONTENTS

INTRODUCTION

Readers who have never heard the radio programme in which these stories were first brought forth are due a word of explanation.

'My Word!' was devised by Tony Shryane and Edward J. Mason in 1956. It is a literary quiz in which the contestants, instead of treating the subject with the usual po-faced reverence, are encouraged to indulge in what Robert Frost called 'perhapsing around'.

For one of the questions on the first show the two male contestants were each given a quotation and asked to explain when, where and by whom the phrase was first used. The quotations were 'Let not poor Nellie starve', and 'Dead, dead and never called me Mother!'. As the first one was too easy, and the second one was a bit difficult to identify as to names and dates, we each invented our answers: (1) 'It was first said by the chef at the Savoy when, late at night and short of puddings, he poured things over a peach, hastily christened it "Peach Melba", and sent it out to a famished Dame Nellie Melba'; (2) 'It was first said by a lad reeling away from a vandalised phonebox after failing to telephone his parent'.

This round became a permanent part of the show and, as the years rolled by, the short explanations grew longer, wilder and more wide-ranging, while the puns at the end - apart from giving pleasure to those listeners who guessed them before we came to them - became less important and more desperate.

And so for a great many years now we have been faced each week with the agony of having to knock out a reasonably coherent story based upon a given quotation - however unpromising the quotation's syllables appeared at first sight.

This volume is a selection of the squeaks produced by the pips being thus squeezed.

F.M. and D.N

But still a pun I do detest,
'Tis such a paltry, humbug jest;
They who've least wit can make them best.

William Combe
Dr Syntax in search of the Picturesque

People that make puns are like wanton boys
that put coppers on the railroad tracks.

Oliver Wendell Holmes
The Autocrat of the Breakfast-Table

BOOK ONE
You Can't Have Your Kayak and Heat It

Mad, bad, and dangerous to know

Lady Caroline Lamb
of Byron, in her Journal

Frank

Now that I am in my fifties, and looking forward to the
first glimmerings of the approach of the beginning of the
first foothills of early middle-age, I can look back, in my
tweedy, pipe-smoking way, to the searingly painful process
of growing up and be glad that it is at last almost over.

I suppose my most traumatic period was when I was
fourteen. A lot of significant things happened to me that
year: my nickname was changed from 'Flossie' to 'Raker',
I became aware of my personal appearance, and I discovered Women - or, to be more precise, Maudie
Thwaites.

Up until this hinge in my life I had been a happy enough
little lad. We lived at Broadstairs and I enjoyed a healthy,
open-air life, losing one sandal every day on the beach and
riding my bike; I had one of the first dynamos, a great
thing the size of a teapot which clamped to the front wheel
with such force that I had to stand on the pedals to get the
bike to go faster than 2 m.p.h. And I was a short, chubby
fellow, addicted to candy-floss - hence my nickname,
Flossie.

On or about my fourteenth birthday a number of
dramatic changes occurred. Almost overnight I shot up
from being five foot one and a half inches to being six foot

three inches, and my teeth started to splay out - hence my new nickname of The Rake, or Raker. Bets were laid at my school on whether I could eat an apple through a tennis racquet.

And I fell madly in love with Maudie Thwaites. With the wisdom of hindsight I can't think why I did this, apart from the undeniable truth that she was there. She was very short indeed, and dumpy with it. She wore spectacles, which she was in the habit of pushing back up her nose with a forefinger about every third second, and she preferred sniffing to having a good blow. And she always seemed to be leaning up against a wall. She would spend whole evenings leaning up against a wall, pushing her spectacles back up and sniffing. I don't think I have ever met anybody since, with the possible exception of the late Mr Maurice Winnick, so devoted to leaning up against a wall. She also kept saying "I'm bored".

It was a period of the most acute agony for me. I had become extremely self-conscious about my appearance, which meant that I was overcome with shyness if anybody even looked in my direction, let alone spoke to me.

I tried to improve my appearance. I went at my hair with fistfuls of solidified brilliantine. To make myself look spotty like the older boys I stuck little round bits of cut-up inner-tube on my chin and neck with fish glue. I persuaded my parents to let me have a brace on my teeth - a device made of gold wire which went round the front of the teeth with two little screws at the back which, when tightened a quarter of a turn every other day, dragged the teeth, squealing, back into the skull. But all to little avail.

Whenever I joined Maud at a wall, all six foot three of me, with my rubber spots and my hair sticking out like a sweep's brush dipped in sump oil, she would just sniff and say "I'm bored". And I couldn't think of anything to say back.

This was partly because I didn't know what "bored" meant. It wasn't a word which had crossed my path before. I thought it meant something like "I'm Belgian". So I would just lean with her in miserable silence for an hour or so and go home. What, I asked myself desperately, does one DO with a woman?

The whole affair might have ended there had not a friend lent me a book. I was quite interested in moths and butterflies at the time and when my friend slipped this book to me and whispered its name in class I accepted it gratefully; I thought he had whispered "Lady Chatterley's larva". On the way home in the tram I started reading it and it wasn't about larva at all. It was about a gamekeeper and a lady in a wood and he was chewing her ear. But what interested me was that the lady liked it. It had never occurred to me that what ladies wanted was not being talked to but something much easier to do - having an ear chewed.

Elated, I sought out Maud and found her leaning up against the Public Library wall.

"I'm bored," she said.

With quiet confidence I leaned down and gave her ear a thorough gnawing.

Now one thing I omitted to mention was that Maud was an ear-ring girl. Some girls are ear-ring girls and some are celluloid slide girls and some are slave-bangle girls. But Maud was an ear-ring girl and that night she was sporting a large, complicated pair made of bent wire in the shape of gladioli.

And as I tried to straighten up - my back was beginning to give - I found that I couldn't. It was as though we were welded together. A moment's panic, a brief exploration, and the ghastly truth was apparent: her ear-ring and my tooth-brace had somehow got twisted round each other and we were fast-lodged.

It was during the ensuing two hours, before we got to Margate General Hospital and the Casualty Officer disconnected us, that I left childish things behind me and became a man. My emergence from the chrysalis was somewhat accelerated by the language Maud used; a string of words entirely new to me - I tried one out on my mother

15

when I got home and she caught me such a cracker with her ring-finger hand that I ricocheted off three walls.

But more than that, Maud's behaviour during that arduous journey opened my eyes to the danger of giving one's affection to a woman before she has proved herself worthy of it. She repeatedly tried to pretend that it was all my fault. My fault! As if *I* had made her wear the fatal ear-rings! And she did nothing but grizzle and complain - and, of course, sniff. She complained when, with a new authority I had somehow acquired, I persuaded old Mr Toddy to cart us part of the way in his wheelbarrow. She moaned at me when cars refused to give us a hitch-hike into Margate - it wasn't my fault, it was the fault of the stuff we had to lie on in the bottom of the wheelbarrow.

And she even carried on when I finally got Mr Parkinson to drive us all the way to the hospital, even though we could lie down comfortably in the back of his vehicle, bracing ourselves against the coffin.

I used to see Maud from time to time after that day and we would chat civilly enough but my passion was spent; I had grown up.

Sometimes, as I was strolling through the town with a younger, more impressionable friend, he would spot Maud leaning up against the wall and ask eagerly, "Hey, who's that leaning up against the wall?"

"That?" I would say, a light, sophisticated smile playing about the corners of my mouth:

"Maud, bored, and dangerous to gnaw."

A nod is as good as a wink to a blind horse

R. H. Barham
'The Ingoldsby Legends'

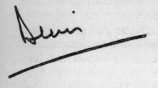

In 1942, I was a Wop. Before I get either a reproachful
letter from the Race Relations people or a Welcome Home
card from the Mafia, let me explain that term. In 1942, a
'Wop' was the RAF abbreviation for 'Wireless Operator',
and that was what Daddy did in World War Two. (Oh,
come on child, you've heard of World War Two, it starred
Leslie Banks.) I was 16 153 58, Wireless Operator U/T: U/T
being another ingenious RAF abbreviation. It stood for
'Under Training'.

About that training. The RAF had calculated that the
maximum period necessary to transform even the most
irresolute of civilians into a red-hot Wireless Operator was
three months. At the time we are considering, I had been
Under Training for a year and a half.

That, again, needs some explanation. You see, before
the RAF would allow you to Operate a Wireless for them,
you had to pass two completely different examinations.
They were both designed to test your skill at reading Morse
Code signals.

The first one tested whether you could read them
aurally. That, if I've spelt the word right, does not mean
through your mouth - but through your ears. What
happened was, you put on a wireless headset and translated

17

any Morse bleeps you heard into letters of the alphabet.

Of the two tests, that was the one I had no trouble with. In fact, I can still do it. To this day, I find myself 'hearing' Morse in all sorts of things. Remember the 'Dragnet theme - 'Dum . . . di-*dum*-dum!'? To my ears, that still comes out as 'Dah . . . di-*dah*-dit', which is Morse Code for 'T.R.' Useful facility, isn't it?

No, it was the second test which, as far as Wireless Operating was concerned, turned me into what we now call a late developer. In this test you had to prove that you could read Morse 'visually'.

Let me describe what that entailed. They stood you on top of a hill, from which you gazed across a valley at another hill. On top of that hill stood the Senior NCO we called 'Fanny', for reasons which memory has blurred.

He operated what was known as an Aldis lamp, a sort of lantern with movable shutters in front. He blinked this on and off at you. The alternations of long blinks of light and short blinks of light formed the Morse Code letters which the RAF expected you, at that distance, to distinguish, translate and write down.

I couldn't even see them. To me, the whole operation was just a vaguely luminous, slightly shimmering blur.

There was good reason for this. A reason immediately apparent to any of you who've ever seen me in that temple of peculiar pleasure, the flesh. The most dominant feature is the glasses with the thick black frames. I wear them nowadays not, as some have supposed, to de-emphasise the deep eye-sockets but to stop me bumping into things. Like office blocks.

In *those* days, however . . . in 1942! Well, I was only going on for twenty, wasn't I? There were girls! I mean, did anyone ever see Robert Taylor wearing *glasses*? Not even when he was playing a scientist.

So that was why, long before the Beatles were even born, I was known to Fanny as 'the fool on the hill'. Never mind not being able to distinguish the blinks of his Aldis lamp - I could barely make out the intervening valley.

I could well have remained Under Training until the Yalta Conference. The reason why I didn't can be summed up in the words of another Beatles' song: 'I get by with a little help from my friends'. Specifically, the other trainees on that 1942 course.

Mind you, it wasn't easy for them to help me. Regulations demanded that the rest of the class stood at least ten yards behind the trainee taking the test - so that no Hawkeye among them could *whisper* the letters to him as they were being blinked out.

So what they did was this. They put themselves in possession of a very long stick of bamboo. 'Liberated' it, as we used to say. Then, as each letter was flashed at me, they prodded that stick into the small of my back. Soft-prod for a short blink of the lamp, hard-prod for a long blink.

If we return to that Dragnet example, in bamboo-stick terms it becomes 'HARD . . . Soft-*HARD*-soft'. Are you with me? So was good fortune. I passed out top of the entry.

Admittedly, I still have to see the osteopath once a week. And, what's more, paying for the visit out of my own pocket. Although I could well present the damaged spinal column to authority as an authentic war wound, to do so might spoil someone else's chances. Because, so I've been told, the ploy is still operating in the RAF.

Even today, RAF trainees who have trouble making out what visual signals are being shone into their short-sighted eyes, are being rescued by that same system of dig-in-the-back simultaneous translation. The lads have even adapted a proverb to cover the situation:

A prod is as good as a blink to a shined Morse.

So he passed over, and all the trumpets
sounded for him on the other side

John Bunyan
'Pilgrim's Progress'

Frank

A few weeks ago the publisher, Mark Bonham Carter, was
walking in Hyde Park when he heard somebody calling his
name, "Mark! Mark!" He turned and there was nobody
there. He walked on a little and again he heard a small
rather querulous voice call, "Mark! Mark! Mark!" Then
he looked downwards and there at his ankles was a small
dog with a hare lip.

I mention the incident as a demonstration of the peculiar
quality which names have for being other things.

I mean, did you know that the Victoria and Albert
Museum was named after two people? Well, it was. It was
named after the men who founded it, Frank Mu and
Alastair Seum.

And take Strip-Tease. Were you aware that Strip-Tease
was named after the man who imported it into this country
at the fag-end of the last century, Phineas Stripp? Well, it
was. It had no name in France but when Phineas imported
the idea he hired a theatre in London in between the
matinee and the evening performance and served tea while
the ladies divested. These became known as Stripp Teas,
and the name stuck.

The story of how Phineas, a poor boy with dreams, beat
the great impresarios at their own game is gripping. Not

very funny, but gripping. Well, not very gripping really; say, semi-gripping.

He had heard tell from travellers that a new form of entertainment was sweeping the halls of Calais and Dieppe. A number of girls were engaged - chiefly from the ranks of unemployed clog-chisellers - and each was provided with a pair of stout, iron button-hooks. Then, to the inflammatory music of Offenbach, the girls stood on stage and proceeded to unbutton their dresses. As at that time the dresses were done up with over three hundred buttons the process took about an hour and a half. The girls then posed for an intoxicating moment in an undershift of bullet-proof mauve bombazine reaching from shin to neck and the customers reeled out into the night air with steam coming out of their ears.

Phineas set to work. He persuaded a theatre manager to lend him a theatre in exchange for two pounds in cash, a second-hand overcoat with a fur collar and first crack at the lady clog-chisellers. Next Phineas had suitable music written for him, on tick, by the composer Hubert Seldom-Byte. His name is not remembered much now but in those days Seldom-Byte was the English equivalent of Offenbach.

It was at that point that young Phineas came up against a snag. His next move was to travel across the channel to Calais and audition a batch of unbuttoners. Although of tender years Phineas had been through the School of Hard Knocks and he had no illusions about the girls: he was fully aware that any unemployed clog-chisellers prepared to parade themselves stark-naked from the shin down and the neck up were No Better Than They Ought To Be, and would need to be carefully selected if he was to get them past Customs.

But he had no money for the fare to Calais.

A lesser man might have given up at this point. For a moment Phineas did contemplate returning to his old job of sprinkling tinsel on coloured picture-postcards of Lord Palmerston but British grit won through. He decided to swim. Or rather, as he could not swim, to float.

It was bitterly cold on Broadstairs beach that morning when, watched by a small group of weeping creditors, Phineas prepared to take to the waves. He had provided himself with twenty yards of string upon which he had threaded eight hundred medicine-bottle corks. With a creditor holding one end of the string, Phineas tied the other end just below his knee then spun round like a tee-to-tum until he had wound himself up in the corks and string. He sang out a cheery farewell, hopped to the water's edge and fell in.

He floated rather well. In a moment the tide had caught him and along the coast he went, his brave figure getting smaller and smaller to the tense watchers on the beach.

Half an hour later his brave figure began to get larger and larger. Just when he was approaching Dover the tide had changed and swept him back to Broadstairs.

The following morning he tried again: the same thing happened. Forty-eight attempts he made that long, hot summer and never once got beyond Dover before being returned by the changing tide.

Then came the breakthrough. One day he was standing next to the plate-glass window of a toy-shop - just reflecting - when he glanced within. There, in the window, a tiny boat was being demonstrated. It skeetered busily around a plateful of water propelled by a tiny chip of camphor at its rear end.

"Europa!" cried Phineas (who had little Greek). "That's my answer!"

In a trice he had purchased from a ladies' outfitters a voluminous undergarment pioneered by Mrs Amelia Bloomer for the use of lady bicyclists. He put double-strength elastic in where the garment gripped below the knees, climbed in, and poured half a hundredweight of fresh camphor balls in at the rear. It was but the work of a moment to wind himself up in the string and corks and totter into the briny.

What a difference this time. There was a fizzing and a bubbling behind him and he found himself zig-zagging erratically round Broadstairs harbour. Fortunately all the Stripp family were noted for their enormous spatula-like feet and Phineas found that by moving his feet this way and that they made a pair of fine rudders, giving him perfect steering control. He straightened up and, to a muffled cheer from the beach, settled down to a steady eight knots on a course of roughly SE by S.

So . . . well, the rest is show-biz history (see *Decline and Fall of the Holborn Empire,* Eddy Gibbon, vol. 4, chap. 8).

So he passed Dover, and all the strumpets undid for him on the other side.

Charity shall cover the multitude of sins

The New Testament
First Epistle General of Peter

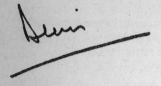

I happened to drop into my club last week - it's the Odeon
Saturday Morning Club, I try to get in there about once a
month - and, while the adverts were on, I got chatting to
the fellow sitting next to me. He made a disconcerting
observation about the way I tell these stories on the 'My
Word!' radio programmes. "Do you realise," he said,
"you have a very . . . slow . . . delivery."

Now that's a strangely uncomfortable thing to have
pointed out about yourself, that you've got a very slow
delivery. It makes you feel a delinquent laundryman. Or an
inexperienced gynaecologist. Although this chap went on
to explain that all he meant was that my mode of utterance
seems inordinately deliberate and emphatic, that only
made me feel worse. You see, I know the reason *why* I talk
like that when on the wireless. And there is no way of
making that reason sound like an achievement.

It's because, on these broadcasting occasions, I am
invariably drunk. Oh, not 'I'll fight any man in the room'
drunk, not even 'I've brought nothing but unhappiness to
everybody who's ever had anything to do with me'
drunk - just 'unless I say this word slowly it won't come
out right' drunk.

It's all a result of something that happened to me about

24

the time I reached forty. Some kind of chemical change took place in my - it's all right, you can do these four-letter words now - body. I don't know exactly what happened but, almost overnight, the absolute minimum of alcohol suddenly became sufficient to start me yodelling. Isn't it terrible to be struck down like that in the prime of life? Without any prior warning, I became a secret non-drinker.

What made that almost a professional disaster, however, was that the alteration in my metabolism coincided almost exactly with the tenth year of the 'My Word!' series. Let me explain the significance of that anniversary: when a radio programme has been on the air for ten years, it thereafter becomes eligible for what the BBC calls 'hospitality'; henceforth, the Corporation provides drinks for the cast before the programme. Mind you, when I say 'drinks', perhaps I should be more precise. Five slim-line tonic-waters, and a bottle of gin which you are allowed to drink down as far as the pencil mark. So there I was, invited at last to drink at the BBC's expense - but, at the same time, rendered physically incapable of accepting the invitation.

Why couldn't I simply stick to tonic-water, you may ask. To answer that, one has to understand the workings of a public corporation. If they were to discover that their bottle of gin was not being drunk down to the pencilled-level indicated, Accounts Department would then embark on what's called 'revising the estimate'. The following week, we'd find the pencil-mark an inch higher up the bottle. And, in Show Business, status is all. The first question any member of one BBC programme asks a representative of another programme is, "How far down the bottle is your pencil-mark?"

"All right," you might acknowledge, "then why don't you just give your gins to one of the other people in the show?" Answer: it would only create worse problems. I mean, which one could I give them to? Certainly not Dilys Powell or Anne Scott-James. Look, you know from films what lady newspaper-columnists are like. Think of Glenda

Farrell, Eve Arden, Rosalind Russell - tough, cynical, suspicious. Way their minds work, any man who starts offering them buckshee gins, he's only after one thing.

Jack Longland, then? No, it just wouldn't be right. You can't offer additional gins to a man who has to drive his wife all the way back to Derbyshire after every programme. It's already difficult enough for him to negotiate those motorways with someone sitting on his cross-bar.

Frank Muir? Oh, come on. . . ! I know Frank's alcoholic reactions as well as I know my own. When he goes on to perform, he is already at the very frontier of his capacity. One more gin and he'd be rolling up his trouser-legs and putting on Dilys's hat.

No, for the welfare of the team, for the sake of the programme, I cannot do other than swallow those gins myself. Even though it results in my performing every show with my upper lip gone numb and my tongue feeling like it's got too large to fit my mouth.

That's the reason for my slow delivery. The only way I can disguise the fact that I have consumed more alcohol than my body can now deal with is to articulate very slowly and . . . very . . . CLEARLY. In the hope that, as the Good Book almost has it:

'Clarity shall cover the multitude of gins.'

And so to bed

Samuel Pepys
'Diary'

Frank

"Oh, botheration!" exclaimed Drusilla Kennington-Oval,
her gamine face puckering at the corners in a tiny moue of
vexation. She had come to the end of her novel,
Heartsease, by Monica Liphook (Olympia Press), and it
was time for her to get out of bed and face another mad,
jolly, gorgeous day.

She widened her slim, artistic fingers, and a thumb, and
the book slipped to the cottage floor with an unaccustomed
plonk. In a trice she was out of bed, long limbs flashing,
and down on her knees mopping up the plonk - a bottle of
agreeable but cheap Yugoslav Chablis which she was trying
out.

It was nearly half-past ten and already she could hear her
farmer neighbours beginning to stir; the slam of a
shooting-brake door as one set off for a round of golf; the
cheerful clatter of helicopter blades as another was
whisked away to some dreary old business meeting in
Brussels.

Not wanting to miss a minute of glorious sunshine Dru
flung on an old pair of patched jeans, thrust her feet into
an old pair of patched moccasins and ran down to her
front gate.

"Hello, Mr Helicopter Pilot!" she cried gaily, waving

both her arms high in the air. "Bon voyage!"

The helicopter hit a tree.

Biting her lip at her silly forgetfulness she ran back into the cottage and flung on an old patched bra and an old patched sweater.

Dru never was much of a one for breakfast. Just a spoonful or two of game pâté flung onto an old Bath Oliver biscuit and she was running like a deer over the familiar hillocks and meadows of Platt's Bottom, breathing in the pure country air - she loved breathing - stopping only for a quick draw on a fag or a chat with a cow.

And then . . . suddenly, there was Derwent Hilliton. A moment before, the lane had been empty. But, now. There was Derwent Hilliton in his new Maserati, forty feet long and nine inches high. Derwent . . .

"Hi, you!" said Derwent, in his usual laconic fashion. He was wiping a speck of dust from the steering-wheel with a ten pound note. Once again Dru was conscious of the sheer animal magnetism which exuded from his every pore. As ever, she caught her breath at his fabulous profile, which he was holding so that she could admire it. There was something almost feminine in his grace of movement as he folded the banknote and put it back into his handbag.

"This is good-bye, Dru," he said, all of a sudden.

"But . . ." gasped Dru, "Why . . .? What . . .? Who . . .? When . . .? If . . .? Could . . .? Is . . .? How . . .? Can . . .?

"Father has just given me a million pounds to make good on my own. I'm off to Tibet tomorrow to build a luxury hotel; the Shangri-La-Hilliton."

"I see. At least, I think I see."

"But it doesn't have to be good-bye. Will you come, Dru? As Mrs Hilliton. Think it over. I'll ring you tonight."

With a muffled roar from the gold-plated twin-exhausts, he was gone.

Dru's heart was in a turmoil; lickety-spit, lickety-spit, it went. Did she really love him? Did he really love her? What to do?

As ever when she was troubled she found that her feet had taken her to Blair Tremayne's cottage, at the back of the 'Dog and Duck'.

And as ever her heart skipped a beat at the simple, bachelor scene inside. An old tennis racquet lying just where he had used it for draining the chips. An old army boot full of cold porridge ready for an early breakfast. The old-fashioned wooden mangle he used for getting the last scrap of toothpaste out of the tube.

For Blair had no father to give him a million pounds. He was just a humble, dedicated writer, hard at work translating a French/English dictionary into English/French. But so kind. And reliable. And . . .

A muffled grunt made her turn, and there was Blair towering over her. He folded her in his arms twice - he had rather long arms - and hugged her tightly to him.

His tweed jacket smelled deliciously of old spaniel dog.

"Dru," he gasped, throatily, "Dru. Oh Dru . . ."

Releasing one hand, he removed an old spaniel dog from beneath his jacket.

"Oh, Dru. Dru."

Blair was a man of few words and had to work those he knew rather hard.

"Dru. Me. And you, Dru. Marry? Eh, Dru? May I be Mr Drusilla Kennington-Oval?"

With a half-cry, Dru freed herself from his dear arms. She had to have time to think. So she walked, and walked. All that day she walked. Through fields, along roads; she knew not where. At one time she thought she recognised the Manchester Ship Canal. Another time she was hailed by a friend in the foyer of the Royal Albion Hotel, Bognor Regis. But she walked on.

When she arrived back at her little cottage there were two bunches of flowers waiting for her. Five hundred orchids tied with satin ribbon bore a card, 'Say yes. Derwent.' Three daisies tied together with fuse-wire bore a piece of tissue paper, 'Be mine. Blair.'

Which to choose? When she opened the curtains on the morning of the honeymoon was she to see the massive glaciers of far-off Tibet? Or an army boot full of cold porridge and a view of the Gents at the back of the 'Dog and Duck?'

Gentle reader, can you doubt her choice?

Dru made her decision. She was wedded and bedded. And on the first morning she flung back the curtains of her bedroom window . . .

And saw Tibet.

It is better to be envied than pitied

Ancient Greek Proverb

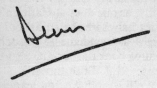

One of the most depressing of middle-life experiences, not that most of them aren't, is trying on your old RAF uniform and finding that the only part of it that still fits you is the tie. That's why my attention perked up at one of the adverts in my local cinema.

'Men!' it said, the exclamation-mark blinking on and off, 'Are you finding yourself with more waist, less speed? Then join our Health Club.' The accompanying visuals displayed a variety of narrow-hipped prematurely-greys vaulting easily over wooden horses, exchanging pleasantries in Our Organic Juice Bar and roaring off in open cars with droopy girls running fingertips up their forearm.

I joined the following day. The name of the Club escapes me now, but it was something out of mythology - 'Priam', or 'Priapus', the kind of allusion that's been popularised by all those classical scholars now on a retainer to advertising agencies for the naming of male deodorants. What I do recall is that the place was a former slaughter-house and that the young man who greeted me wore one of those thick roll-neck sweaters I still associate with U-Boat captains. He also had the kind of handshake that ought never to be used except as a tourniquet. It took me a good four minutes to get my knuckles back in line.

31

His first move was to sell me, for a price I would normally expect to pay for a winter overcoat, a pair of gym shorts and a cotton singlet. After I'd changed into them, I presented myself before him for inspection. All right, admittedly not an impressive sight but, for heaven's sake, hardly deserving the performance he put on.

"Oh dear, oh lor," he kept repeating. He was walking round me slowly and respectfully, as one does at Hadrian's Villa or Pompeii, any of the places where the guidebooks use the phrase 'ruined grandeur'."Oh you have let yourself go, haven't you," he said finally.

"I have," I said. "And I enjoyed it. Both times."

"Not to worry, old-timer. We'll soon have you leaping about again. Be the fittest sixty-year-old down your street.

"I'm forty-six," I said. But by this time he had me in among the rest of the class.

Well, I don't like to appear condescending, but honestly, repulsive really is the only word. Not one of them could have been a day under forty-eight or fifty. Watching all of them wheezing about in those baggy shorts and the singlets with 'I Am The Greatest' across the chest, I couldn't help but give the U-Boat captain a rueful wink, which he affected not to notice.

No one can say that, over the next hour, I didn't co-operate fully in all that bend, stretch, lift, pull, lie flat, run on the spot, up-up-up-up, everybody jump on everybody else's back. Nor did I fail to pull my weight during all the succeeding Wednesdays and Fridays that I joined the old crocks there at what I soon came privately to refer to as 'Hernia's Hideaway'.

I even did, twice a day in the privacy of my office, the special P.T. homework which the Club asked of me. As instructed, I bent forward, grasped the ends of my two feet firmly and, without letting go, did pull-pull-pull for a full quarter of an hour. As far as I could tell, the only noticeable result was that, two months later, I'd gone from a size ten shoe to a size twelve.

It was not till he got me on to weight-lifting that

breaking-point was reached. Holding between his thumb and forefinger a thick iron bar with two enormous discs at either end, he said, "Righto then, your turn."

I looked behind me. "It's you I'm talking to," he said. "The Phyllosan Kid. Let's see a standing snatch. Take your time."

I won't have anyone accuse me of not trying. I spat on my hands, bent down, took a firm grip, jammed my back-teeth together, tightened my stomach muscles, bore down on my heels, and did a sharp, powerful snatch. For eight minutes. At which point he said, "Not bad for first time. Friday we'll see if you can lift it as far as your ankles. Go and have a shower now."

I put a question to him. "Have you got the kind of shower that has its nozzle in the ground, so that the water squirts vertically upwards?"

"What do you want one of them for?"

"Because I can't straighten up."

No more could I. Well into the autumn I was still moving around in a kind of Groucho Marx lope. If Physical Training is the price you have to pay for Physical Fitness, I'll settle for pooped. Those Ancient Greeks knew what they were talking about:

It is better to be unfit than P.T.'d.

The lamps are going out all over Europe

Edward, Viscount Grey of Fallodon
3 Aug. 1914

Frank

The Most Unforgettable Character I ever met was - well,
he's dead now and I don't remember much about him. On
the other hand, the Most Forgettable Character I ever met
is most memorable. He was elected Most Forgettable
Character by our form at school. The craze for electing the
Most Something-or-other had hit our form heavily that
year - I was, I recall, elected the Most Smelly, an injustice
which has rankled ever since. But the application of the
word 'forgettable' to Oliver Sinclair Yarrop was only too
appropriate. I can see him now, a veal-faced lad with no
colour about him anywhere; his hair was the same colour
as his skin, which was colourless; he had almost transparent ears. He took no interest at all in the normal
pursuits of healthy schoolboys, like boasting loudly,
spitting, eating, punching girls: his sole passion in life was
the love, and care, of animals.

It is a melancholy fact, which as schoolboys we but
dimly perceived, that Dame Fate is a cruel Jade; and one of
her little caprices is to allow a growing lad to work up a
lifetime ambition whilst at the same time making sure that
he is totally unequipped to achieve it. Thus my best friend,
Nigel Leatherbarrow, wanted to be the Pope: he was
Jewish. And my second-best-friend, Tarquin Wilson,

wanted to be a girl. And I wanted to be rich. But the worst example was poor little, Forgettable Oliver; he desperately wanted to be a vet, and as much as he loved animals, they loathed him.

I, interested in people but indifferent to furred and feathered beasts, was beloved by the animal kingdom. Even now I cannot walk very far before dogs appear from nowhere and sniff my socks. When I return home I find a nest of field mice in my turn-ups. I have only to pause a moment to lean up against a tree and ladybirds settle on me in such numbers that I look as if I have galloping chicken pox.

But all animal life viewed Oliver with implacable hatred. Full of love for them, he would hold out his left hand for every dog to sniff. When he left school the fingers of his left hand were an inch shorter than those of his right hand. Every pullover he possessed was lacerated by kittens' claws. One of his jackets had lost a shoulder where a cow had taken a bite at him. His right shin bore the scar where a chicken had driven her beak in. Animals had bitten him so much that when I saw him, for the last time, stripped for gym, he looked deckle-edged.

I did not see Oliver again until after the war. I was at an RAF hospital in the country being treated for shock - brought on by the realisation that I was about to be demobilised and would have to work for a living - and on a country walk I suddenly came upon Oliver. He had his back to a brick wall and was being attacked by a duckling. Unclamping the bird's beak from Oliver's ankle I fell to talking. He had changed considerably since we last met. He no longer wore his school cap and long trousers covered his bony, unmemorable knees. He seemed middle-aged before his time. He had on one of those gingery, very thick tweed suits with bits in them which look as though they had been woven from marmalade. His hair was very thin; almost emaciated. And he only had one arm.

It seems that he gave up all hopes of becoming a vet when he realised that the exams meant maths. But an aunt died, leaving him a little money - she was a member of an obscure religious sect; he assured me that she had returned to earth and still lived with him in the form of a stuffed airedale - and he had decided to spend the rest of his life in tending animals in an amateur way. For that purpose he went for little walks, always carrying with him a thermometer and a used lolly-stick so that when he encountered an animal he could make it say 'Aaah!' and take its temperature. It was work he loved.

But, he confessed with a sudden flush, he had not as yet managed to examine an animal. No sooner had he pressed his used lolly-stick on the little, or large, or forked tongue than the creature sank its teeth into the nearest available piece of Oliver and was away. Not one 'Aaah!' had he achieved.

And worse than that, a blow from a robin's wing had lost him his arm. Oliver was up a ladder at the time, trying to take the temperature of this robin who was on a branch of an apple-tree. Apparently Oliver thought the robin looked rather flushed so approached it with his lolly-stick and said "say 'Aaah!' " whereupon the robin flapped a wing which dislodged an apple which fell on Oliver's fingers and he let go of the ladder.

Less obvious but just as regrettable was the loss of his left big toe when the tortoise he was trying to examine fell from his hands, and the loss of two medium toes on his right foot due to circumstances which I did not quite grasp but which entailed a rabbit and Oliver wearing green socks.

That was the last time I saw what was left of Oliver alive. I read an account of his passing over in a local paper I was folding up the other day (I had a hole in my shoe and it was coming on to rain). The newspaper report said that Oliver Sinclair Yarrop had bent down with a lolly-stick to a young lamb and was trying to persuade it to say 'Aaah!'. What Oliver had not noticed was that there was a large goat just behind him. But the goat had noticed Oliver. And the temptation was too great. It had charged.

As the coroner said, it was not the butt which hurt Oliver

so much as the landing, which took an appreciable time to occur during which time Oliver was accelerating at the rate of thirty-two feet per sec. per sec. But what did the deceased think he was doing, fooling about with a lamb on the edge of Beachy Head?

So the Forgettable Oliver died, and is almost forgotten. But if there is a hereafter, and I think there is, he will be happy at last. There will be green fields there. And hundreds and hundreds of little woolly lambs.

And more than that:

The lambs are going 'Aaah!' to Oliver Yarrop.

Oh the little more, and how much it is

Robert Browning
'By the Fireside'

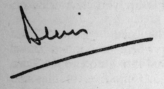

Some time ago Frank Muir and I wrote a television series which turned out so dire that one newspaper considered reviewing it in the obituary column. The comment which caused Frank most distress, however, appeared in a Sunday rag. 'It is now obvious that Muir and Norden have exhibited themselves so frequently as performers, they no longer possess any ability to write. They are now to be regarded merely as talkers.'

I cannot recall ever seeing my colleague more choked. "Do you realise," he said, "do you realise the implications if what that paper says is true? Bang go my chances for Posterity. And you know how I feel about Posterity."

I do. He's very keen on it. "When I go," he said, "I want to be remembered."

"Well, I'll remember you," I said. "I bet I will. Burly chap with a bow-tie. Swiped my felt-nib pen."

"Nobody'd call you Posterity, would they? I'm talking about real *afterwards* Posterity. 'Merely talkers!' What a shameful rotten thing for a paper to write. Name me one 'talker' who's been remembered by Posterity. Eh? Name me one! Yes all right, Dr Johnson. But he had Boswell, didn't he? All I've got is you."

Frank is inclined to do that. Ask you a question,

38

answer it himself, then tell you you were wrong. This time, however, something different happened. He suddenly sat up an stared at me. Then - "Sir," he said. "Sir, it may be that you will suffice."

He had never called me 'Sir' before. Within the tundra of my heart, something thawed and started trickling. "Dear old Frank," I said. "What are you chuntering on about?"

"Boswell and Johnson," he said. "Boswell just followed Johnson around everywhere and jotted down every observation Johnson uttered into a notebook. Then he transferred all the notebook stuff into five volumes and came up with *Boswell's Life Of Dr Johnson*. One of the all-time Posterity chart-toppers! Well, why can't you do the same thing?"

"Because," I said. "I think he's dead. We could check with the British Medical Council, but they must have so many Dr Johnsons on their - "

"Sir," Frank said. "Follow me more closely. *Norden's Life of Mr Muir!* Using exactly the same technique. By cracky, the more I think about it, the more I like it. Can you give me a good reason why we can't start right away?"

"I think so," I said. "I haven't got a notebook."

"Sir," Frank said, and one could tell he was already living the part. "Sir, you will need more than one notebook. Five volumes at, say, three hundred pages per each, let's see." He stabbed expertly at his pocket-calculator. Then he took it out of his pocket and stabbed again. When we'd checked the answer with my Ready Reckoner, we set off for that Office Stationery shop in Maddox Street. The manager, I thought, seemed a little anxious when we explained ourselves.

"Sir," Frank said, not only living it now but loving it. "Sir, I am Frank Muir and this is my biographer. Do you stock those 3p notebooks with a spiral wire going up and down the spine?" We had agreed that those would be the best form of notebook for me to carry, as they wouldn't spoil the shape of my good suit when accompanying Frank to coffee-houses or journeys to the Highlands.

"I think I can find you one," the manager said.

"Sir," Frank said, "eight hundred and seventy."

One thing about that manager, he did help stack the eight hundred and seventy notebooks inside a wooden crate, in order to make them easier for me to carry. I say 'me' because, as Frank pointed out, if he were to give a hand in the humping about of a dirty great wooden crate, how would he have the puff to utter any observations for me to copy down.

As we tauntered back along Regent Street - 'taunter' is a labour-saving word I'm using to describe the appearance of one person sauntering, the other tottering - so clement and agreeable was the autumnal sunshine that Frank was moved to utter Observation One.

"Sir," he observed, "could the fact that new cars are invariably introduced in the autumn be the reason why they are sometimes known as autumnobiles?"

Unfortunately, the blood was now pounding so hard in my ears, I didn't hear what he said. "Do what?" I asked.

"I just did an observation," Frank said.

"Sorry. Hang about." I lowered the wooden crate to the pavement and took out the top notebook. "Sir," Frank said, "could the fact that new cars are invariably intro-duced in the why aren't you writing any of this down?"

"You've still got my felt-nib pen."

He threw it at me. "Get it down while it's fresh."

I wrote feverishly then stopped. "I didn't really hear what you said." A few people had now gathered round us. "Please," I said to Frank, "just one more time."

As he reiterated it, very slowly this time and quite loudly, I wrote it carefully into the notebook. While I was doing so, a small elderly lady plucked at my sleeve. "Excuse me, Officer," she said. "What are you charging him with?"

Now it must have happened during the time I was explaining to that lady that I was not a plain-clothes policeman, I was a biographer just starting on the first page of the first notebook of a five-volume biography, it must have been while I was busy doing that that some alert mafioso swiped the wooden crate.

That is the reason why the publication of the not-much-heralded *Norden's Life of Mr Muir* has been unavoidably delayed. The fact is, all I have of it do date is one measly observation and a bill for eight hundred and seventy spiral wire notebooks at 3p each which comes to a sum of no less than would you believe £26.10. As Browning damn near got round to commenting:

'Oh, the little Muir, and how much it is!'

I was desolate and sick of an old passion

Ernest Dowson
'Non Sum Qualis Eram'

Frank

I have rather gone off Denis Norden. One does go off people from time to time. Other people I have been off (off whom I have been?) include Crippen, Hitler, Mrs Mary Whitehouse, Pontius Pilate, Patrick Campbell, Professor A. L. Rowse and Charlie Chaplin, so Denis is in good company. It's just that he was a bit infuriating this afternoon.

We had arranged to meet at his office at 3 p.m. on a matter of business - he was trying to sell me a camera which he had dropped - and when I arrived at seven minutes past the hour he said to me, with a trace of irritability in his normally suave voice, "You're late."

Well, I mean to say. He was the cause of it. Just as I was leaving home I received this garbled message from his secretary, Hedda Garbler, saying that Denis had been having lunch at a Chinese restaurant and had left something there which belonged to his aunt and would I pick it up on my way in and thank you.

Ever the one to oblige an old friend I dropped in on the restaurant and collected the thing, of which thement was visibly glad to be relieved, which appeared to be a rolled-up, dark grey, very tatty sheepskin rug - and rather smelly with it.

I proceeded blithely along Kensington High Street in an easterly direction, playing with the thing the way one does when carrying a thing - tossing it in the air and catching it, punting it along the pavement for a bit, shoving it under the arm and carrying it like a rugger ball - when I realised that it was giving off warmth. This was a little alarming so I stopped and began to unwrap the bundle. Or rather, I tried to unwrap the bundle. It was not a bundle. Or a rolled-up rug. It was a very, very old, mangy Persian cat.

Now I am not a cat man. I am unable to exchange minds with a cat. Sigmund Freud spent thirty years researching into the feminine soul before confessing that he could find no answer to the question: what does a woman *want*? I feel the same sense of inadequacy with a cat.

I looked at the cat and the cat returned the favour with a steady look of cold, implacable malevolence.

I decided upon a show of strength.

"All right, Moggy," I said firmly, "let's go."

She gave a sort of sweep with one arm and my hair had four partings in it.

Cats have these scimitars built into their paws for just this sort of aggro and my old lady had hers locked in the 'attack' position. A sharp pain in my side told me that she was putting in some serious work on my jacket - obviously trying to get at my liver.

In a flash I grabbed her by the neck and stuffed her into my jacket pocket. I left her head sticking out so that she could breathe but by clamping my hand against the pocket I had her tightly pinioned.

"Get out of that!" I chortled.

I felt her go rigid. I realised later that she went rigid when she was thinking things out; planning her next move.

It came just as I was about level with the Albert Hall. My right thigh began to grow hot. Then it grew cold. And my right ankle felt distinctly damp.

She had gained the initiative once again.

Hoisting her out of my pocket by the neck and holding her at arms length I nipped into that little ironmonger's shop near Albert Hall Mansions, bought a ball of shiny string, tied one end round her neck and paid out the string until I had her on a ten-yard-long lead. My thinking was that by the time she had run that ten yards, scimitars bared, I would have had a chance to take evasive action.

She was furious. She immediately went rigid, pondering, and I was able to make quite a bit of distance, dragging her along on the end of the string.

She got my measure just as we came up to Hyde Park Corner. There was a quick flurry of fur and she emerged out of her trance like a streak of lightning, tearing round and round me in a clockwise direction. I couldn't think what she was up to at first but I soon found out. In a moment she had me trussed up in string like a mummy. I teetered for a second, trying to keep my balance, but, very gently, she gave a little pull on the string and I crashed to the ground.

I extricated myself from the string and then it was I who went rigid. After some thought it seemed to me that I should not attempt the impossible, i.e. to outwit the cat or overcome it by strength, but to concentrate on solving the immediate problem: how to prevent myself from being wound up in the string and brought crashing to the pavement every few yards. As the cat acted - I would have to react.

And so that is how we proceeded along the length of Piccadilly and into Denis's office, in a kind of screw movement; the cat sprinting round me in a clockwise direction while I sprinted round the cat in an anti-clockwise direction.

I arrived at seven minutes past the hour and he said "You're late." Can you wonder that I have gone off him?

Indeed I was late. But I was a little more than late.

I was dizzy, late and sick of an old Persian.

Hope springs eternal in the human breast

Alexander Pope
'Essay on Criticism'

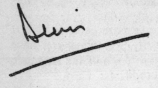

If you saw some months ago, a rather tangled version of this quotation headlining *The Times* music critic's column, I'm afraid that was my fault. It was the outcome of an incident where I saved a young Dutch girl from being mowed down by a runaway hors d'oeuvre trolley.

What happened was, I was having lunch with an American producer who'd had the idea of making a film called *Marty*, to be based on the life of Luther. And while he was going on about it, I saw an hors d'oeuvre trolley start to move forward.

Now as you know, in elegant London hotels the hors d'oeuvre trolleys are always about the size of small trams. As, at this place, the dining-room floor also had a slight incline, once the trolley got rolling, it gathered speed at an enormous lick and, in no time, was hurtling down the room, rocking and swaying and spilling out Russian salad and sardines.

Then I noticed something else. Directly in its path was this girl. To make matters worse, she happened to be bending forward - not consciously, I don't think, she just had rather heavy ear-rings on. Anyway, without even thinking, I dived forward and swept her aside. The great trolley hurtled past and splattered itself harmlessly against

45

an elderly waiter. (A team of surgeons, I've been told, were still picking black olives out of him six hours later.)

The girl's husband, a prosperous Dutchman, was quite embarrassingly grateful. Apparently, they'd only been married three days and were having a week's honeymoon in London. So if the trolley had claimed her, it would have been a really rotten waste of a double room.

"Mijnheer," he said to me, with more emotion than I had thought the Dutch capable of, "for what you have done, I will send to you the largest token of my gratitude that my craftsmen can manufacture."

All right, what would you have reckoned he had in mind? So did I. Cupidity glands started extruding like icing-bags. Seven complete days passed before it was borne upon me that diamond-cutting is not the only craft for which the Dutch are renowned.

The reminder came from the man from British Rail Services. When I opened the door of my flat to him, he said, "It won't go in the lift and I'm not humping it up them stairs."

I accompanied him down to the entrance hall and there it was. A cheese. A Dutch cheese, the size of - look, do you remember that cartwheel Bernard Miles used to lean on? Well imagine something the same diameter, but about two feet thick and bright red.

I stood gazing at it for quite some time. As it happens, I am allergic to cheese. It dates back to an incident in my boyhood when I pulled on a pair of swimming trunks, inside which someone had left a loaded mouse-trap.

So I said to the van man, "Can't you possibly take it away again? Share it out among the lads?"

He turned out to be one of those people who talk in A's and B's. "A," he said, "I'm not ruining myself trying to lift that thing up again, B, how would anyone cut it?"

It was then I had a brainwave. In Flat 14, there was this young musician, a student of the Royal Academy of Music. And what was he studying? The Harp.

Do I need to spell out the rest of it? After all, in

existential terms, what is a harp but an oversized cheese-slicer with cultural pretensions?

In the event, it worked a treat. The van man had no trouble carrying the Dutch treasure away in lightweight slices and, no doubt, his depot is still acclaimed for the lavishness of its wine-and-cheese parties.

And that should have been the end of the story. But unfortunately - and I honestly do feel badly about this - that very night the young music student had arranged to give his first recital. A test piece by Schumann, at the Rudolf Steiner Hall.

I blame no one but myself. Even today, I still don't know whether it was the after-effect of the van man and me sitting so heavily on the frame of the harp to force the strings through the cheese; or whether it was just that cheese itself exerts some kind of emancipating effect upon harp-strings.

All that anyone knows for certain is, on the eighth bar of the Schumann piece, when the young man from No. 14 grabbed a handful of strings and then, as is the way in harp-plucking, released them, they all flew out of the harp and struck a gentleman in the fourth row, a retired colonel who'd wandered in under the impression it was going to be that lecture on 'How To Cure Stammering'.

It's not a sequence of circumstances of which I'm in any way proud. But if relating it has done nothing else, it may have helped clear matters up for those of you who still puzzle over the headline which appeared the following morning above *The Times* music critic's review of the performance.

'Harp Strings Hit Colonel In The Schumann Test.'

'Old Soldiers Never Die'

Song. 1914-1918

Frank

The other morning I was sitting over my breakfast egg - I hadn't finished my toast and marmalade and I didn't want my egg to get cold - when my wife suddenly said, "Do you know what I was doing exactly ten years ago this morning?" I raced back down Memory Lane. It was empty.

"No, what?"

"I was sitting in the top room of a Genoese watch-tower in Corsica, writing postcards under an umbrella."

She was right. As I retrieved the egg from beneath me and started digging into it, memory flooded back. Of course - the priest and the eggs!

Ten years ago we bought a sort of mediaeval potting-shed in the hill village of Monticello, which sits six hundred feet above the small port of Ile-Rousse. We went out and moved in exactly ten years ago, on Easter Monday.

In no time we had the place shipshape; fresh newspaper on the table; packing-case lined with straw for the children to sleep in; and our own bed made up in a little room across the bridge, which was the top part of an ancient watch-tower. Pleasantly fatigued after all that, we strolled across the square to the bar for a quick Casanis, a Corsican aperitif based upon, I think, torpedo fluid and marine varnish. The first sip had hardly started corroding the fillings before the bad news was broken to us.

It seems that you must never sleep in a house in Corsica before it has been blessed by a priest.

And more than that, there must be coloured eggs in every room to be blessed.

And so the awful chain of events began. There was not an egg to be had in the village, brown white or variegated, and the shops were shut for the holiday.

Things were getting a little desperate and I couldn't think what to do next, apart from shout at the children, when I noticed some vaguely egg-shaped pots lying about. They were about a foot high and made of dirty-white earthenware. Apparently the villagers filled them with soil and grew things in them, like geraniums and carrots. We bore six of these off to our place and set about getting some colour into them. We boiled up my wife's new blue dress in a bucket, steeped the pots in that and they came out quite a pleasant pale blue. We steeped the other three in hot beetroot juice and they took on a fine mauve tinge. We had our coloured eggs. Now for the priest.

The nearest priest lived in Ile-Rousse, which was down three miles of hairpin bends. I borrowed a car from the man next door and set off. It was one of those tiny Citroens which the French are so fond of; they are made of corrugated iron and cock a leg going round corners. As the layout inside the car was totally alien I decided not to risk using the engine and just gave the thing a shove, jumped in and coasted all the way down to the port.

By the time I had located the priest and persuaded the priest to come up to Monticello - a triumph of diplomacy; he was ninety-two and had earache - it was dark. And it began to rain. Now Mediterranean rain differs from British rain. You don't get it so regularly but when you do it is bigger, faster, wetter, and it bounces higher.

It was when we were in the car, with the stuff pounding down on the roof, that I realised that I had no idea how to put the car into motion. Starting the engine was simple enough, merely a matter of turning the key. But the gears . . .

Citroen 2CVs don't go in for a gear-lever, as one understands a gear-lever. Instead, there is a white toffee-apple sticking out of the dashboard. And there is no indication anywhere as to which way the thing has to be turned, bent, lifted, pulled, inclined or thrust in order to locate first gear.

I wrestled with the toffee-apple for quite a long while, with the priest sitting quietly beside me mumbling to himself in Latin, when suddenly, we lurched backwards. I had found reverse.

I resolved not to push my luck any farther, and backed gently towards Monticello.

All went well within the street lights of Ile-Rousse but once we had started reversing up the steep, twisted road to Monticello two things became apparent: a car's headlamps point forwards not backwards, and although windscreen wipers keep a driver's vision clear in the heaviest of rain there are no windscreen wipers on the rear window.

There was nothing for it but to ask the priest to get out and walk ahead of the car to guide me.

It took nearly an hour to climb the hill and I must say that it was a very tired, sodden and cross priest indeed who allowed me to propel him into our residence.

"There you are, Father," I said, with a sweep of the hand. "Coloured eggs as per instructions. Bless this house."

But something had gone wrong. The 'eggs' were no longer coloured. In the two hours I had been absent the colour had completely faded from them and they were clearly just six earthenware pots, albeit egg-shaped.

"Ostrich eggs, Father," I mumbled, without hope. "Colouring very pale . . ."

He broke into words. "These are not coloured eggs. These are jars which the villagers fill with soil to grow things like bougainvillea and turnips."

"Now you come to mention it, Father," I cried, fighting

to the last, "they DO look like jars used for growing things in. A fantastic resemblance . . ."

It was no use, of course. He wasn't fooled for a second by our anaemic pottery. The last we saw of him was his frail figure making for the bar.

So our house was not blessed.

And during the night a wind rose up and stripped half the tiles from the tower roof. And the rain continued to rain.

And next morning, when my wife wrote her postcards home, she had to do so sitting in the tower under an umbrella.

The irony is that I would never have made such a pathetic attempt to deceive the old priest if I had known then, as I know now, an ancient Corsican proverb:

'Old soiljars never dye.'

'Forever Amber'

Title of Novel
Kathleen Winsor

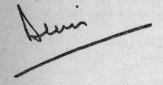

Once in a lifetime, every scriptwriter gets an idea that really fires him. In my case, from every film-studio that I've approached with it. But this idea, I pledge you, this is the blockbuster, it's the big one. What makes me so sure is - and isn't this always the real test? - I can outline the whole idea in just five words. Three, if hyphens count. A peace-time war-film!

What do you mean impossible? Will you just *listen!*

When you get right down to it, what is a war-film? Isn't the story always the same one? Some kind of mixed group - a fighter squadron, say, a commando platoon, a squad of marines, doesn't matter - an assemblage of individuals from all walks of life who finally, under the stress of combat and danger, learn how to work together as one unit? Right. So here's what to do. We take a peace-time equivalent of that kind of group and - now follow me here - we tell their story in exactly the same kind of terms.

I know what's going through your mind. What kind of peace-time group in any way resembles a group of war-time commandos, marines, fighter pilots? Okay, try this on for size. A Formation Dancing Team?

Suddenly gone quiet, haven't you? So let me fill the story in, just broad brush-strokes.

We open, like all those war-films do, at the place where 'it all happened'. But - as the place looks *now*, present day. Abandoned, empty, deserted. In our case, it's a ballroom. An abandoned, empty, deserted ballroom.

Into it wanders our hero. No longer a young man. Touches of grey here and there. But still looking good, of course. Sexy. Slowly he walks across the empty ballroom - we do the echo-thing with his footsteps - then he pauses. Looking down at the maple dance-floor, he rubs his shoe on its dust. As the camera moves in on his face, into his eyes comes that look that tells us he's going to have a flash-back. Far-off sounds creep in! Shuffle of patent-leather shoes, rustle of taffeta dresses, chickychickybomchick of a samba. As they get louder, louder, the whole screen goes sort of ripple-y - and when it clears up again, boom, we're in.

It's ten years ago - and there they are. The Mrs Eva Swaythling Formation Dancing Team. Six men, six women. The Clean Dozen. Heading them up - the Skipper. Mrs Eva Swaythling herself! Hardbitten, loud-mouthed, ruthless. Joan Crawford if we can get her, if not we go for Charles Bronson.

She's barking out orders. "I'm going to make dancers out of you if it means you rhumba on the stumps of your ankles!" Tough as they come, see? But, underneath it all, deep down - golden syrup.

Cut to cameos of each of the team. John Mills, the spoilt rich kid who finally learns humility. Richard Atten-borough, the lovable cockney. ("Time for a brew-up, Skipper?") Sarah Miles, whose puppy is dying and medical science is baffled. The coloured boy, you can do this now, the coloured boy who turns out braver then anybody. Susan George, who gets raped by a second-trumpet player, but off-screen so we keep the U Certificate.

The Mrs Eva Swaythling Formation Dancers. . . . We do a montage of their training. Mile after mile in quickstep tempo, carrying 250 lb of sequins on their backs. The pitiful shortage of equipment. "How are we gonna get the material for the girls' dresses, Skip . . .?" "Give us the tulle and we'll finish the job."

Their first night-op. The Hammersmith Palais during a power-cut. We show their triumphs, we show their reverses. And not only their reverses, their chassis-turns, their scissors-steps. And always, right out there in front, Mrs Eva Swaythling. Threatening, cajoling, exhorting, "There are no atheists in a foxtrot."

Finally comes the this-is-the-moment-that-all-your-training's-been-the-preparation-for moment. They're going in against Jerry. It's the Eurovision Area Championships.

They're in the dressing room of the Streatham Locarno. Waiting. "It's quiet out there. . . ." "Too damned quiet. I don't like it. . . ." "Time for a brew-up, Skipper?"

Crash of sound - and they're plunged into the maelstrom! Into the shrieking, pounding bombardment that is the Ken Mackintosh Orchestra. Thrills! Spills! Chills! In the fourth sequence of the Military Two-Step, the Number Three man suddenly staggers. His shoe lace has snapped! But, like a well-oiled machine, the two girls either side of him move in and, without breaking step, support him between their puff-sleeves. He finishes the flower-pattern on one shoe!

It looks like nothing can stop them. But then, just as the Latin American heat starts - tragedy! Mrs Eva Swaythling winces, claps her hands to her iron bosom. Her face contorts. The Souvenir Brochure slips from her nerveless fingers. . . .

Around the' ballroom the word flashes. "Mrs Eva Swaythling's bought it!" In that great dance hall in the sky, there'll be a new pair of silver shoes tonight.

Momentarily the Team falter, become ragged. But it is the coloured boy who rallies them. "Okay, gang. Let's get this one for the Skipper!"

The ballroom will never see Formation Dancing like that again. And, as the samba chickychickyboms to its climax, the Mrs Eva Swaythling Team realise they've done it.

They've brought the Common Market Latin American Area Trophy back to Britain. . . .

Must be a milestone in screen history. Eh? Must be. There's only one thing that's still holding me up on it, apart from the fact that everyone thinks it's rotten. Finding the right title for it. *In Which We Swerve?* . . . *Last Military Two-Step In Streatham?* . . . Nuh.

No, I think there's only one title that captures the sweep and majesty of the story - that broken rallying-cry which snatched victory from the jaws of Latin American defeat. How does this grab you? . . .

'For Eva - Samba!'

'Supercalifragilisticexpialidocious'

Title of song from 'Mary Poppins'

Frank

The pure unalloyed joy, the flight of the heart on wings of song, the flowering of the spirit like the opening of a jacaranda-tree blossom at the prospect of my wife returning tomorrow after a week away is tempered by the thought of the squalid state the kitchen is in.

In order to preserve the balance of nature it is vital that I maintain the fiction that I am capable, at a pinch, of looking after myself and can be left for a few hours without change and decay taking over the household.

So, in the few hours left me, I have an alarming number of important things to do, most of which have been brought about by my firm conviction that women run things on old-fashioned, traditional lines which would benefit from the application of a cold, rational, male intelligence; i.e. mine.

First of all I must replenish the stock of tinned soup in the store cupboard. Round about Day Two I realised that man could live on tinned soup alone. It heats up in a jiffy and, more than that, the tin can be used as a throwaway saucepan. With the help of a pair of pliers to hold the thing, the empty tin can be used to boil eggs or anything else and then thrown away; the soul-numbing process of washing-up is thereby minimised. The trouble is that a keen female eye, viewing the stock cupboard, will spot at a glance that a suspicious quantity of tinned soup has been consumed. So it must be replaced.

On Day One I had realised that, as master of all I surveyed, I did not have to eat vegetables. I have no religious or moral objections to vegetables but they are, as it were, dull. They are the also-rans of the plate. One takes an egg, or a piece of meat, or fish, with pleasure but then one has, as a kind of penance, to dilute one's pleasure with a damp lump of boskage. However, this puritan attitude that no meal is worthy without veg. is strongly held in this house so I must somehow give the impression that vegetables have been consumed in quantity. What I must do is to buy a cauliflower and shake it about a bit in the kitchen. Fragments will then be found under the table and in corners, giving the impression that vegetables have been in the forefront of my diet.

And then there is the refrigerator. This seemed to me a most inefficient instrument, yielding up stiff butter when I wanted it to spread, ice-cold milk when I wanted milk to warm up for the coffee, and when I needed some ice cubes the ice container was apparently welded to the shelf with cold. So I instituted a system whereby I switched off the fridge at breakfast, thereby making the contents malleable when I needed them, and switched it on again at night. This has worked quite well except that the contents of the fridge are now a cluster of variously sized rectangular snowballs. I must remember to take a hammer and chisel to them before tomorrow.

And I need a stout elastic band because I have done in the vacuum cleaner. I used one of my gumboots for kitchen refuse to save messing about with a bin but liquids seeped through a hole in the toe. The obvious solution to a hole in a gumboot toe is to bung it up with a mixture of sawdust and the remains of that tin of car undersealing compound which one has in one's garage. I poured the underseal and the sawdust into a thing called a Liquidiser, which is a kind of electric food-mixer, but what I failed to

57

note was that one is supposed to put the lid on before operating it. And when I began to vacuum clean the mixture of tar and sawdust off the kitchen ceiling it seemed to jam up the works. The motor went on running but there was a smell of burning rubber and now I must, before tomorrow, provide the vacuum cleaner with a new rubber band.

And eggs. We have an ark in the orchard containing nine hens, which provide us with a regular intake of beige eggs. I went out to feed them on Evening One and I think that they missed my wife. They greeted me, I felt, reproachfully, making sounds not unlike those made by Mr Frankie Howerd. "Ooh!" they went, "Ooooh, OooooOOOh." So I undid the door of the ark and led them on an educational tour of the garden, pointing out where the new drainage is to be laid, the place on the lawn where I had lost my lighter, the vulgar shape which one of the poplar trees had grown into. And then the dogs joined us and helped to take the chickens out of themselves by chasing them, and soon the air was filled with feathers and joyous squawks. I finally got the chickens back into the ark by midnight but, oddly, they haven't laid an egg between them the whole week. Since my wife will be expecting to be greeted by about three dozen beige eggs, I must do something about this before she returns.

I also had a spot of bother with a packet of frozen peas. I thought I would vary my diet by making myself a Spanish omelette, i.e. as I understood it, an omelette with a pea or two in it. Now the packet stated clearly that if less than four servings was required the necessary amount could be obtained by giving the frozen pack a sharp buffet with an instrument. I had my soup tin on the gas-stove, with a knob of butter in it, and I obeyed the instructions; that is to say, I held the frozen lump in my left hand and aimed a blow at it with a convenient instrument - my dog's drinking bowl. It worked up to a point. One frozen pea detached itself, bounced off my knee, and disappeared. Where had it gone? My Afghan hound was right next to me at the time, watching keenly what I was doing with her bowl, and I had a sudden horrible suspicion that the pea had gone into her ear. I called to her. She evinced no interest. I went round to the other side and called again. She looked up. I made a mental note to take the dog to the vet for a swift peaectomy operation before tomorrow.

Lastly there is the problem of my breath. Last night I made myself a casserole of sausages - or rather, a soup-tin-role of sausages - but I seemed to have lost the salt. After a deal of searching I found an alien-looking container marked 'Sel' and applied it liberally. It seems that it was garlic salt. I did not realise what it had done to my breath - one doesn't with garlic - until this afternoon when I stood waiting for somebody to open a door for me and suddenly noticed that the varnish on the door was bubbling.

So I have a number of things to remember to do tomorrow, such as tinned soup, a cauliflower, de-frosting the refrigerator, buying an elastic band for the vacuum cleaner, getting in three dozen beige eggs, seeing the vet about the pea in the dog's ear and taking something for the garlic on my breath.

How, you are perhaps asking yourself, will he possibly remember all these things?

Well, hopefully I have put them all together into a kind of chant, or song. It goes:

'Soup . . . a cauli . . . fridge . . .elastic . . . eggs . . . pea . . . halitosis.'

'Great Expectations'

Title of Novel
Charles Dickens

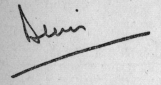

If it's true that we laugh loudest at that which we hate most, then my favourite joke is the one that Ronnie Scott tells about the fellow who says to a girl "Do you like Dickens?" and she says "I don't know, I've never been to one." Because I just can't be doing with Dickens. It's some kind of blind spot, I'm sorry, he holds out nothing whatever for me. That's why, if it hadn't been for a story in this morning's newspaper, the above quotation would have put me in a right hiatus.

It was a story about smuggling immigrants into Britain. As you must know by now, there is, in this ancient seat of freedom, a growing body of organised apoplexy which refuses to believe that immigration is the sincerest form of flattery. Consequently, a minor but lucrative hustle has grown up, based on smuggling persons of foreign origin across our frontiers at a hundred and fifty pounds a nob.

Well, according to the newspaper story, one clever youngster hit on a bright variation. He loaded sixteen Asian nationals inside a large wooden crate, drilled the necessary air-holes, then had the crate flown Air Freight to Heathrow. The intention was that once a lorry had off-loaded it into the Freight Shed, he would then, prior to Customs inspection, prise open the crate and assist its occupants to effect a stealthy exit through the Spectators' Car Park.

And had it not been for the uncertain state of industrial relations at London Airport, it would have made an exemplary essay in Creative Smuggling. The crate was off-loaded from the plane, all right. But just as the lorry was about to take it to the Freight Shed, a twenty-four-hour strike was called.

The driver slammed on his brakes, switched off the ignition, climbed out of his cab and scampered off to join his colleagues harmonising 'We Shall Not Be Moved' hard by the Departure Lounge. In consequence, the crate of sixteen Asians was left at the far end of the runway until such time as the twenty-four-hour strike finished.

Well, another fact of life that will not have escaped you is that, in this country, the twenty-four-hour strike is like the twenty-four-hour 'flu. You have to reckon on it lasting at least five days.

This proved about three days too many for the crated Asians. On the second day, they held a whispered consultation. That, in itself, is no easy task when you're packed in layers of four. By a show of hands - again, not easy - they agreed that further confinement might prove too irksome to endure. So, using a system of co-ordinated inhaling and exhaling, they burst open the sides of the crate.

Too bad, really. They were immediately apprehended by the Chairman of BOAC. It just so happened he was taking a stroll out to the far end of the runway to try to get away from the sound of Clive Jenkins' voice.

Sad, isn't it, typical of the times in which we live, all goes to show, etc., etc.

Far as I'm concerned, though, if it hadn't been for the Heathrow Sixteen's resentment of the prolonged incarceration, I'd never have found that newspaper sub-head which circumvented my Dickensian block:

'Crate Irks Packed Asians.'

'Ta-ra-ra-boom-de-ay!'

Title of Song

Frank

I propose to tell you pretty well all there is to know about an animal which is very popular among dog-lovers though less so among dog-haters. I refer to the dog. Dogs, like horses, are quadrupeds. That is to say, they have four rupeds, one at each corner, on which they walk. In many other ways dogs are like horses - for example, they both like eating biscuits and being photographed and being tickled behind the ear - but they are not all THAT much like horses because they are smaller. Except, of course, if you match a very huge dog indeed up against a tiny, tiny horse who hasn't been well, when it is quite difficult to tell the difference between them.

If you find yourself in the predicament of facing a very large dog and a tiny horse, not knowing which is which, the wisest thing to do is to wait until they are both moving towards you then shout "whoa!" The one that doesn't stop is the dog. This is a reasonably safe test unless the name of the horse is Woe, in which case they will both approach. Or the horse is deaf.

Dogs are very historical, some of the earliest being found by Marco Polo up Chinese mandarins' sleeves.

The Romans had dogs and named the Canary Islands after them, although this was by way of being a bit of a mistake: the Romans had very, very large and hairy canaries and very, very small yellow dogs and they got the two mixed up.

Much mention is made of dogs in English literature. The popular dog's name, Prince, comes from Shakespeare's *Hamlet,* where Prince was a Great Dane. From the same play comes a popular doggy expression "Down, Prince!" uttered by Ophelia.

Another reference occurs in *Macbeth*. A dog misbehaves himself in the castle and Lady Macbeth, very cross, cries "Out, damned Spot!"

Keats mentions a dog in one of his longer poems but I can't remember which one.

Elizabeth Barrett Browning had a King Charles spaniel which sat on the end of the sofa with her and helped her pine for Robert Browning but it did not have a memorable name.

Bill somebody-or-other in a novel by Charles Dickens had some sort of dog - I think it was a black-and-white one - but I've forgotten its name.

That is all I remember about dogs in English literature.

There is a large selection of various sorts of dogs for those interested in acquiring one. Poodles are very popular because they do not moult, or run amok and get their names in the paper, and they would much rather be people than dogs so - except twice a year - they do not bother much with each other. Poodles usually come in three shades, black, white and brown, though not all at once. Black ones are nice in that they don't show the dirt but when they sit down in the shadows they are invisible and you tend to tread on one by accident causing you to pitch forward, graze your knee on the radiator and end up with your elbow in the potatoes.

The Chow is a large, hairy dog with eyes rather like raisins and a mauve tongue which is the same mauve as that wine-gum which when you come to it you cover with your thumb and stop handing them round. They are very popular in Italy where a song was written to a Chow puppy: 'Chow, Chow, Bambino'.

Another large dog is the Afghan Hound, which looks like a greyhound in a fun-fur. Afghans are very beautiful. They eat meat, biscuits, fish, books, chairs, bicycle tyres, mattresses, carpets, tables, raincoats, trees, car upholstery and milkmen.

Greyhounds were once much more popular than they are nowadays, perhaps because they need so much exercising. Very few men are willing, after a hard day at the factory bench or in the boardroom, to arrive home and then take the greyhound out for its run, and many middle-aged men find it increasingly difficult to squeeze themselves into the trap.

Flat-dwellers in the modern world are turning increasingly towards smaller dogs and small dogs are becoming extremely popular. The smallest of all is the Chihuahua, a naked Mexican animal the size of a pound of stewing steak.

Not surprisingly, the Chihuahua is supplanting the bigger dogs in the affections of pet-owners. It is very difficult indeed to mistake a Chihuahua for a horse. It requires very little exercise - a swift daily trot round the back-door mat suffices - and it could live happily in a telephone-box let alone a small flat. So no wonder the latest copy of the trade journal, *The Doggy Times,* carried a banner headline:

'Chihuahua Boom Today.'

Now is the time for all good men to
come to the aid of the party

Edwin Meade Robinson
'The Typewriter's Song'

For the thinking man, there is much to be learned from
that piece of advice printed on most bottles of patent medi-
cine: 'Keep Away from Small Children'. Personally, I've
always avoided them as much as possible. However, when
the child is your own and it's her fifth birthday party. . . .

It was an illuminating experience, if repulsive. One
moment a tiny shy thing, in her party dress, had her hand
in mine, waiting for the first of her little friends to arrive.
A ring at the front door - then this bulldozer hurled past
me, wrenched the door open and with a "Where's my
present, where's my present?" shoved the small guest up
against a wall and frisked him from head to foot. It is
something of a jarring moment when you realise you have
brought another Customs Officer into the world.

"She's over-excited," I muttered to the boy's mother.
But that lady's gaze had already swept past what was going
on in the hall and was busy in the kitchen, pricing our
units.

Ten minutes later there were twenty-three guests present.
I spent quite a while watching the little boys at play. What I
found interesting was not so much that early defining of
sexual roles about which there's so much chat-show chatter
these days, more how the actual playing of the role has

altered since my time. When I was that age, small boys used to point pistols and say, "Bang, bang, you're dead." Now they point pieces· of plastic and say, "Zap, zap, you're sterile."

While I was having a ponder on that, I felt a tug at my trousers. It was one of the little girls. "I'm Caroline."

"I know, dear. So's practically everybody."

We had eight Carolines present. Eight Carolines, five Rebeccas, four Jakes and about half a dozen Jamies. Where have all the Harolds and Muriels gone? Who was the last child to be christened Sadie? Caroline said, "Do you like my new dress?"

"It's lovely, dear."

"I'm wearing a bra."

True as I'm sitting here. Didn't come up as far as my knee-cap. Don't you find something chilling about someone wearing uplift before they've got any up to lift? I had the greatest difficulty, the rest of the afternoon, restraining her from showing it to me.

Her persistence was only diverted by the announcement that tea was to be served. The tea also proved to be what Jimmy Durante used to call a revolting development. Talk about eat, drink and be messy. Has science ever explained why, at that age, the only time they sneeze is when they've just taken a mouthful of sponge cake?

But it was after the meal that the really interesting problem arose. There is one lesson to be drawn from it that I can pass on to you immediately. When giving children's parties, never serve eight jugs of orangeade in a house which has only one bathroom. What you are immediately brought up against is the myth that the British are united by a common language. It was one of the Simons who came up to me first. "Mister," he said, "I want to go soo-soo."

I narrowed my eyes at him. "You want to what?" But the fattest of the Rebeccas was now pulling my sleeve. "Yes, dear?"

"Where do I tinkle?" she said. As I stared at her

blankly, a rather red-faced Jake came dashing in. Very fast. "Make whistle-whistle," he announced. Urgently.

"Look, children," I began - but, at that moment, the most soignee of the Carolines entered the room. "I want to go to the loo," she said.

The penny dropped. I turned back to the original Simon, the one who'd uttered the first request. "Hear that, lad?" I asked him. "That's what you should have said. 'I want to go to the loo.' "

"Not any more," he said.

What has the education explosion really achieved, I wondered to myself later that evening as I was rubbing away at the carpet. What kind of society is it where parents have narrowed the range of names which their children can be christened down to little more than half a dozen, while at the same time creating an infinity of names for the potty?

What's needed, I decided, is a standardisation of appellation in the second area. And it's needed right away, before we all disappear down the generation gap. What I suggest is a Royal Commission - headed, preferably, by someone of the stature of Lord Goodman - to decide on one official phrase to which everybody's children will then conform.

If you're with me on this, please send S.A.E. You will receive by return a sticker for the rear window of your car:

'Now Is The Time For Lord Goodman To Come To The Aid Of The Potty.'

They bore him barefac'd on the bier

William Shakespeare
'Hamlet', iv.v.

Frank

I wonder whether you share my delight in Fanny Hill? I find it really pretty there in the Spring, so easy to get to from Godalming by bicycle and there is a lovely view from the top if you stand on your saddle. I was doing just that some five years ago when I detected that something was amiss. "Hello, Frank," I distinctly remember saying to myself as I balanced precariously with one foot on the saddle, "all is not A.1 at Lloyd's."

The reason for my perturbation was that I seemed not to be seeing quite as much of the lovely countryside as I was accustomed to see: the lady who took her Sunday afternoon bath at exactly four o'clock in the small cottage two hundred yards beyond the hedge was still visible. But only from the neck up.

I pondered. Either the thicket hedge had grown sharply since the previous Sunday thus cutting off the view, or I had shrunk slightly.

I checked. Bicycle against the same telegraph pole. Same shoes. Socks no thinner; the same hand-knitted heather mixture. Then I saw. My rear tyre was quite flat. I had a puncture.

No problem, of course, to a practical man. I levered the tyre off with the tablespoon I always carry with me for my hourly spoonful of Queen Bee honey, licked round the inner-tube until I detected the bubble and started to apply the tube of sticky stuff. Then happened what frequently happens when, for instance, one is faced with a particularly intricate crossword puzzle clue - the solution did not immediately present itself. I squeezed the tube, jumped on it and bit it but it was hopeless; the stuff inside had perished. I resolved to seek help. Lying some way back from the road was a house I had often noticed when I was idly waiting for four o'clock to arrive; an odd Victorian gothic residence set about with fruit trees and a croquet lawn.

The door was opened by a prim, middle-aged maid, clad in the uniform of her kind. She dropped a little, old-fashioned curtsey and murmured that she would inform the master. As I waited in the hall, contemplating the mezzo-tints of past-Presidents of the Royal Philanthropic Society, my mind was troubled. There was something about the maid that was curious, unusual. But what? "Come along, Frank," I remember saying to myself, "there's something about her that's not all tickety-boo." Then I realised what it was. She had a vast spade beard.

At that moment another woman, visibly the housekeeper, came in to say that Mr Pennithorne Phipps would see me. She was middle-aged, dressed in black, and her beard, though luxuriant, was a faintly fictional shade of auburn. Perhaps - who knows a woman's wiles - aided by a dab from a bottle?

Mr Pennithorne Phipps, a kindly, elderly man, received me affably, gave me a tube of rubber solution and a glass of cloudy sherry and insisted on telling me his story.

As a comparatively young man he had inherited a large sum of money which he resolved to put to some good purpose. A close friend, after trying unsuccessfully to sell him a gold-mine in Basingstoke, reluctantly accepted this philanthropic intent and advised him to do what he could to alleviate the plight of circus folk, who were being put out of work in their thousands due to people being more interested in the wireless and the cinema than in going to the circus.

Young Pennithorne Phipps set to with a will, which had been through Probate and had made him a very rich man indeed. He persuaded motor-car manufacturers to hire the India-Rubber Men to demonstrate how simple it was to get in and out of their smaller cars. He talked restaurateurs into engaging the Lilliputian Midgets to sit in their restaurants and so make the servings look bigger. He hired the Human Cannonballs to seaside landladies - after the flight was timed the landlady could legally advertise 'Only one minute from the sea'.

But he could find no work for four bearded ladies. They were shy of other people. It was obviously too dangerous for them to go into industry and have to bend over lathes or sewing machines. Their chances of a modelling career were slim. So he decided to take them into his house to look after him. And this they did most delightfully, one gardening, one cooking, one housekeeping, and one maiding. And in the long winter evenings, when the shadows drew in, they would plait each other's beards with pale ribbons on the ends of which were little wooden balls. Then the four of them would bend over their dulcimers and, with little twitches and nods of their heads, play for him the airs he never tired of hearing, like Corelli's Concerto Grosso in G Minor, and 'Put A Bit Of Powder On It, Father'. And when he was down in the dumps and *triste* they would amuse him by playing Beard Football, which was like Blow Football but instead of blowing down tubes to urge the ball into the goal the ladies tried to sweep it in with their beards.

That was five years ago. I never returned to the house, nor to the hill, because of a serious accident which befell me a few minutes after leaving the house. I mended my puncture and took up my usual position on tiptoe on the saddle, observing the scenery. All was as usual. The lady enjoyed her bath, as did I, until, quite unexpectedly, the lady did something most imaginative with her loofah and I fell off the bike.

The hospital did what they could but it was a complicated fracture. "Give it to me straight, Doctor," I said. She paused for a moment, then said, "I live in a cottage about two hundred yards from a hill - you won't have heard of it - Fanny Hill. It's only a weekend cottage - I go there for a rest, and a bath, on Sundays - but I love that little hill. I'm sorry . . . but you will never be able to cycle up any sort of hill again."

Nor have I. But last week a friend lent me his light van for the weekend and I had a sudden urge to recapture the pleasures of those Sundays five years ago. I drove to Fanny Hill. As I had ten minutes in hand before four o'clock I, on an impulse, called at the old Victorian gothic cottage.

What a change I found. The door was opened by the same maid - but she was clean shaven, and she smelt very strongly of brown ale.

"Dunno where he is," she said, and left me.

I glanced behind me. The lawns were lumpy and the croquet hoops were mottled with rust.

A noise made me turn back. It was the housekeeper descending the stairs; the last two on her behind.

"Hang on, cock," she said, "I'll fetch the old fool."

She, too, was clean shaven.

It was a sad Pennithorne Phipps indeed who faced me. It seems that he grew troubled about his four bearded ladies shortly after I had last seen them. Although they were entirely content he felt that perhaps he was being selfish in keeping them within the confines of the house. So he brought a specialist man down from London and paid for him to remove their beards by electrolysis. They were now normal women, able to take their place in society.

"It's been frightful," he said. "They troop down to the village every evening; they spend most of the time in the pub downing gallons of brown ale . . . there's no dulcimer playing . . . they can't now . . . nor Beard Football . . . instead of being happy, perfectly adjusted people they have become quarrelsome, competitive and, well, just plain dreary. They are now very dull people indeed."

A few minutes later, as I took my aluminium ladder from the back of the van, adjusted it against the telegraph pole, got myself comfortably into position, binoculars at the ready, I thought over the sad story of Pennithorne Phipps and it seemed to contain a moral: Kindness is a lovely thing, but too much kindness can, in a funny way, corrupt.

Poor Pennithorne Phipps's ladies. Bearded and out of the ordinary, they were delightful people. But now . . .

They bore him - bare-faced, on the beer.

The least said, soonest mended

Charles Dickens
'The Pickwick Papers'

This is the phrase on which the Glastonberrys have based
their lawsuit against the ground-landlord. Tell you about
the Glastonberrys. They're our local monied couple. Rich,
rich, rich. Mr Glastonberry has some sort of corner in flag-
pole manufacturing, a small-boned man whose life seems
dedicated to the proposition that Neatness Counts. He
always looks so exceptionally dapper, the local theory is
that she keeps a plastic cover over him when not in use.
Mrs Glastonberry is all Wedgwood hair and lipstick on the
teeth, the sort of woman who asks for the wine-list in a
Wimpy Bar.

Their passion is houses. They buy and discard houses as
though on a winning streak in Monopoly. Over the past ten
years, they must have lived in eight different houses, each
one featuring some conspicuously exotic adjunct of
gracious living. One house had a conversation-pit, another
a barbecue-terrace. I can remember an indoor ski-slope, a
set of pornographic stained-glass windows, a pelota
court . . .

But it was the novelty-item in her latest home that
brought on the lawsuit. "Do come and see our new pad,"
she called to me in the Washeteria soon after they moved
in. "We got it because of the sauna."

73

That statement was true, as has since been revealed, in a very exact sense. It was only by reason of the sauna that the house had come on the market at all. The previous owner had perished in it.

Poor old soul, it was one of those chance-in-a-million situations. He'd entered it - if you've never seen a sauna, it's like a sort of sweating-hot garden-shed - he'd turned the temperature up to about 120 degrees, lolled about till he was the colour of shrimp-cocktail, then gone to open the door to go out for a cooling shower. The handle of the door had jammed. . . .

I must say, when Mrs Glastonberry recounted this to me that evening, my keenness to enter the sauna waned. "Oh, it's in perfect working order now," she assured me. "The landlord's had it repaired. We made that a condition of the lease. But, anyway, Walter insists that he should be the first one to try it."

Walter is the son. A somewhat unhealthily complexioned fifteen-year-old, who always puts me in mind of one of Krafft-Ebing's footnotes. What my Mother calls 'sly'.

He came bustling up with a towel round his middle. "Mother," he said, "if we want to do this right, we've got to do it the Scandinavian way."

"What's the Scandinavian way, dear?"

"Mixed."

They have this au-pair girl galled Gia. A rather striking-looking Italian, who walks as though she never exhales. Mrs Glastonberry looked disconcerted.

"Oh, Mum, don't be a wet. It's only ten minutes. For heaven's sake, if a thing's worth doing - "

Enter Gia wearing a towel that started late and finished early. Walter took her hand, and they entered the sauna. It's a converted cupboard under the stairs, really, which the poor old previous owner had lined with lead and had a special kind of stove put in.

We waited outside it, sipping drinks and munching squares of toast which had been smeared with foodstuffs of such unidentifiable blandness, they were a kind of gastronomic Muzak.

After about half an hour, uneasiness was noticeably prevalent. "Are you all right in there, Walter?" Mrs Glastonberry called, tapping on the door with her solitaire.

"Mum, the handle's jammed again."

Consternation. "Harold," said Mrs Glastonberry to her husband, "your fifteen-year-old son is locked in there with a nude Italian!"

After some consideration, Harold said, "And think of the heat."

We tried opening the door from the outside. It rattled a bit but didn't budge. Five of us got our shoulders together and charged the door. Not a hope. Lead-lined, you see, for the insulation.

"Mum," came Walter's voice, "Gia's fainted."

"Move to the far side of the sauna immediately," said Mrs Glastonberry.

"Don't worry, Mum," Walter said a moment later, "I'm giving her the kiss of life."

He continued giving it to her, according to my Timex, for the next hour and a half. At midnight, someone suggested we fetch the Vicar and try to persuade him to marry them through the keyhole.

Five minutes after that, the door opened and Walter and Gia emerged. They looked, as newspapers say, little the worse for their ordeal. Looked, in fact, all things considered, extraordinarily cheerful. Another note I made, but nobody else seemed to, was that on emerging Walter extracted a key from the inside of the door and slipped it under his towel.

It was when the Sicilian relatives started coming over for the wedding that the Glastonberrys instituted their lawsuit against the landlord for failing to carry out stipulated repairs. Personally, I think they've got a good case. After all, as Mrs Glastonberry keeps trying to translate into Italian:

"The lease said sauna's mended."

Ring down the curtain, the farce is over

Rabelais's last words (attributed)

Frank

I was in the morning room. I shouldn't have been in the morning room because it was half-past two in the afternoon, but I couldn't go into the sitting room because I wanted to stand. Or, to be more accurate, I wanted to walk. And the sitting room is hardly the place in which to walk, let alone stand.

It was my desire to walk backwards and forwards. I much prefer walking backwards and forwards because it saves turning. I walk forward as far as I can go - usually until the tip of my nose comes to rest against the wallpaper - and then I walk backwards as far as I can go - usually indicated by the back of my head gently bumping against the wall. I then proceed forward again and repeat the process until I have walked enough.

If, on the other hand, I turned when I reached the wall rather than reversing, then this would mean that the sole of my right shoe would wear out more quickly than that of the left - I find that I usually turn on my right foot - which would lead to difficulties when the right shoe became due for repair at a time when the left shoe was still serviceable.

The need to reverse rather than turn was further strengthened by the fact that I was carrying an anvil in my right hand. The weight of this would have considerably accelerated the wear on the sole of the right shoe.

I had passed a length of stout rope round the anvil, leaving a loop by which to carry the thing. It was this loop that I was holding by the right hand as I walked up and down the morning room that afternoon. I was carrying the anvil because I wished to make my right arm half an inch longer - I had bought an inexpensive tweed sports jacket the right arm of which was half an inch longer than the left.

After perhaps an hour of walking a friend of mine, a retired tee-planter - he used to be a golfer's caddy - came in to see me. They say that the definition of a friend is someone to whom you don't feel obliged to speak. My friend sat watching me for an hour in silence, and then left.

Shortly after that I heard my wife calling. I put down the anvil and made my way into the drawing room where I found my wife quietly drawing. She is quite artistic and has made a fine collection of English kitsch which she has on display in the kitchen.

"Yes, my love?" I began, when I suddenly noticed with mounting horror that neither of her feet was touching the ground.

I started forward, but a closer examination revealed that she was lying on the sofa.

"Why is there a hole through the drawing room wall just by your chair?" she asked. "Did you make it?"

"Indeed I did!" I said warmly. "With a hammer and a cold chisel only this very morning."

"Why did you knock a hole through our drawing room wall?"

"Quite simply, my love, to enable me to play the bass flute should I ever wish to take it up. You will notice that my chair is hard up against the wall and that the wall is on the right of the chair. If the urge ever came upon me to learn to play the bass flute I now have enough room to the right of me - an essential prerequisite of bass flute-playing just as enough room in front is necessary to a trombonist."

"Yes, but the wind blows straight through the hole and the rain comes in. Surely there is something you can put over the hole until you decide whether or not to take up the bass flute?"

"Good thinking, my dear," I said. "You know what would answer the purpose if we could lay our hands on one - a framed aquatint of Lowestoft Harbour showing the Old Groin."

It took us days to find one.

Then in came this auction catalogue of the village road-sweeper's effects. He had won the pools and bought the Uffizi Palace in Florence so was selling off his former possessions in five lots, namely, lot one - a gas ring, circa 1952, with a faulty tube; lot two - a pile of down useful for stuffing pillows; lot three - a double-damask curtain of great age which did him in lieu of a front door; lot four - his sole article of furniture, a rickety Victorian sofa covered with carved squiggles and ornaments; and lot five - a framed aquatint of Lowestoft Harbour showing the Old Groin.

I hurried round to the auction-room with a feeling that destiny was on my side. The man there said that lot five would come up at about a quarter to four, so I was in plenty of time.

Bidding started briskly for the gas ring. It had reached 5p when I thought I had better check the time. Now I wear my watch on my right wrist to confuse thieves and I was wearing my new, inexpensive sports jacket with the overlong sleeve. I put my arm up and wriggled it so that I could read the time on my watch and found that I had bought the gas ring.

This was most vexing. But even more vexing was that exactly the same thing happened with the pile of down, the double-damask curtain and the fussy Victorian settee. And when the auctioneer did get to lot five - the aquatint - I had no money left to buy it.

I trailed miserably home and found my wife busy doing some sums in the summerhouse.

"Well?" she said, eagerly. "Did you bid?"

"I did," I replied.

"And did you buy it?"

"I bought," I said, picking my words carefully. "But not it."

"Now look here, Rover," said my wife, using the pet name she always applies in moments of anger, "just what have you bought?"

In a very small voice I whispered:

"Ring . . . down . . . the curtain . . . the fussy sofa."

His word is as good as his bond

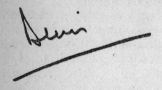

Full-frontal nudity - and there's as catch-penny an opening as you'll ever see - has now become accepted by every branch of the theatrical profession with the possible exception of lady accordion-players. There is, however, one group of performers whom it threatens to relegate to the status of an endangered species. Conjurors.

It takes but a moment's reflection to realise why. Think of all those live doves, lighted cigarettes, steel rings. Where, with no clothes to secrete them *in,* is a conjuror to produce them *from?* A naked conjuror is at as much of a disadvantage as a vegetarian vampire or a cautious lemming.

That's why my heart went out to Nigel Gascoyne, Society Illusionist. Particularly as he was already under a bit of a cloud, following an unfortunate lapse of concentration during his 'Sawing A Woman In Half' illusion. "Oh, it's a swine of a trick, that is," he confided to me afterwards, "if you allow your mind to wander for even a *second . . .*" Fortunately, the mishap didn't prove fatal and the lady concerned is now living contentedly in Scarborough. And Devon.

But the ensuing publicity, coupled with the growing public hunger for more and more nudity in entertainment, meant hard times for Nigel. From the elegant purlieus of London's glittering West End, he was reduced to performing in cheap Holiday camps, convalescent homes for the more obscure diseases, TUC Conferences . . .

"You just got to find a way of sexing-up the act, Nigel" his agent kept saying. "It's flesh they want these days."

"From a *conjuror?*" Nigel said bleakly.

But remonstrance was futile. The downward drift continued. Gradually he found himself performing to smaller and smaller audiences - The Clarence Hatry Dividend Club, the Vladivostok Young Conservatives, the ITA Opera Appreciation Society. . . . Piece by piece, he was reduced to selling off his equipment, the very tools of his trade. The interlocking steel rings went to a scrapmetal merchant, the doves to a pacifist rally, the fifteen tied-together multi-coloured silk handkerchiefs to a Property Developer with hay-fever.

By Christmas Eve, all that remained of that rich diversity of exotica which Nigel had been wont to produce from about his person was one egg - a pathetic relic of his 'disappearing an egg from inside a black velvet bag' illusion. Oh, it had been a sensation in cabaret, that illusion. The awed murmurs that the egg's disappearance used to evoke from highly-placed executives at Management-By-Objective banquets! ("Surely he must be a devotee of witchcraft, a follower of the left-hand path?")

But life is not always a cabaret, old chum. Today that egg was all that stood between Nigel and starvation. Alone in his squalid bed-sit, he gazed at it, wishing there were only some way he could cook it. Oh, there was a gas ring by the grimy wall - but he no longer had the wherewithal to replenish its greedy slot. "That's show-business, all right," he reflected bitterly. "When a 10p piece for the meter is beyond the means of someone whose very name is Gascoyne."

Perhaps he could kindle a fire in the grate with his faded press-notices? But would they burn strongly enough to boil an egg? Probably not. Something more solid in the way of fuel was needed. A piece of wood of some kind? A piece of wood. . . .

Can there be a more tragic symbol of surrender than a conjuror burning his wand? The wand, after all, is at the very heart of the conjuring experience. A wandless conjuror becomes, almost by definition, as incapable of function as a deaf lumberjack (can't hear TIMBER!) or a bow-legged wine-waiter (can't hold the bottle between knees for pulling cork out).

Or so one would have said. However, in a nearby room of that dingy lodging-house, crouched another practitioner of the performing arts: a former strip-tease artist named Alice B. Topless. She also had become a casualty to the sociological malaise which Veblen has called "conspicuous display", but she preferred to describe as "too much bleeding amateur competition".

Now - alone, penniless, starving - she was contemplating putting an end to it all by impaling herself on a portable TV aerial. But as she moved towards it, she suddenly paused - sniffed. So sharpened by hunger had her senses become, her delicate nostrils had detected, drifting across that sordid hallway, the aroma of boiling egg! Timidly, she went out into the hall and tapped on Nigel's door . . .

Today 'Nigel Gascoyne & Alice - The Daring Deceivers' are a show business legend. Did I say a conjuror without a wand is incapable of functioning? That must now be qualified. What we failed to consider was the *purpose* of a wand. Why does a conjuror make such play with the wand when tapping it sharply against the rim of a black velvet bag? For only one reason: to draw your eyes away from what his other hand is groping for inside the recesses of his tail coat. In other words, the wand is only there to 'misdirect', to distract the audience's attention.

Bearing that in mind, suppose now that, instead of a wand, your conjuror has an extremely beautiful bird standing at his side. And, at the point in the illusion when he wants all eyes diverted away from him - at that exact moment, every stitch of that bird's clothing *falls to the ground?*

All requirements are satisfied, aren't they? The moral seems to be that, these days, a nude lady-assistant can serve a conjuror's purposes every bit as effectively as his little bit of wood used to. Or, as Alice herself puts it:

"His bird is as good as his wand."

The Law is not concerned with trifles

Old Legal Maxim

To His Honour, The Chief Judge,
The Centre Court,
Old Bailey,
London.

Dear Honour,

No doubt you wondered why I did not present myself, as the policeman told me to, at your court last Wednesday at 10.30 inst. to answer the charge which had been levelled at me, viz. and to wit as under. Namely, that I did heave, with malice aforethought, a quantity of hot food over the personages of Lord Ickenham, Lady Ickenham, the Hon. Ickenham and their three guests, causing them to sustain distress, a bill for dry-cleaning and, in the case of Lady Ickenham, half a pint of hot gravy down the cleavage.

The reason I did not turn up for my trial, Your Worship, lies in the circumstances as follows.

Until the day before the occurrance occurred I had been, by profession, unemployed. Then I saw this advertisement that a waiter was required for the restaurant up the Post Office Tower. Your Grace probably does not eat out much of an evening what with having to wear that wig and the funny clothes and being laughed at by other diners so I will

84

fill you in a bit about the restaurant. It resides, as I said, five hundred and ninety feet up the Post Office Tower. It gives a pretty view over London and the menu is about four foot square.

I arrived for my appointment with the manager an hour and a half late and had to have a lie-down before he could ask me any questions (I have since learnt that it is possible to get to the top by lift), but he decided that as he was so short-handed he would give me a try-out and I was to start immediately.

What he forgot to tell me, what with me being late and lunch having started and the tables full of rich people looking out of the windows and saying "That must be Highgate", was that the restaurant revolves.

This is a most important part of my case, Lord. I should have been told that the restaurant revolves. It is not - I maintain - a normal thing for a restaurant to do and unless one is given the nod beforehand one's natural expectancy is that the place will stay put.

How it works is like this. The whole thing is circular, that is to say, round. The kitchen and the Ladies and Gents and the wine cellar and so on are in the middle. In a sort of circular core. Round this is a perimeter, about twelve feet wide, on which are the tables. It is this outer ring, with the people on it, which revolves. It does not whizz round at a great lick, My Honour, or the eaters would be flung out of the windows and scattered all over Soho. It revolves very slowly so as you hardly notice. And I should have been told.

I emerged from the kitchen and at the first table in front of me was Lord Ickenham's party. I adjusted the carbon in my pad, briskly noted their first order, which was for soup, about-turned and walked straight into the Ladies. I covered up as best I could by mumbling "Sorry gentlemen" and found my way back to the kitchen next door, but it was an unnerving experience; the two rooms seem to have changed places behind my back.

I put six bowls of soup on a tray and headed out again.

But Lord Ickenham and party had apparently got fed up with waiting and left. At their table was a party of Japanese tourists. They did not want soup so I turned to go back to the kitchen and found myself in the manager's office. By now I was beginning to feel ill. I returned to the Japanese to find that they too had left and the table was now occupied by a jolly party from Uttoxeter who gave me a huge order for spaghetti and asparagus with butter sauce and roast beef and fish.

By the time I had realised that all was not what it seemed to be, so I walked very carefully through the door which I *knew* was the kitchen. It was the wine cellar. The kitchen proved to be right round the other side of the curved wall of doors. I loaded up my tray with the mass of food ordered by the Uttoxeter party and emerged cautiously from the kitchen. . . .

Imagine my surprise, and delight, to find sitting seated at the table in front of me my original party, consisting and comprising of Lord Ickenham, Lady Ickenham, the Hon. Ickenham and their three guests.

I was so pleased at things returning, as it were, to normal that I rushed forward to greet them, bearing the loaded tray above my head.

This, I now realise, was a mistake. For one thing it is never a good policy to rush forward bearing loaded trays. For another thing, there is a join where the bit which revolves meets the bit which stays put. Not a huge join, but just big enough a join for one's toe to catch in.

Suffice it to say, Your Lord, that I tripped and my whole trayful of hot nosh deluged Lord Ickenham and party - particularly Lady Ickenham.

Quite naturally I fled the scene. I rushed for the manager's office to offer him my personal resignation. But it was not the manager's office which I entered. Once again something had happened to the geography and what I entered was, in point of fact, the service lift. Or more precisely the service lift-shaft, the lift itself being at ground level at the time.

And that is why I was unable to be with you at the trial last Wednesday, and why I am writing this from my hospital bed. The surgeon said I was very lucky in that I fell on my head and I should be out and about again in a month or so. I will certainly pop in and see My Lordship when I am my old self again.

But in the interim I would like to point out, Worship, that I do not think that Lord Ickenham has a case. I am sure that I do not need to remind Thee of the rules which govern English Courts of Justice, and have done from time immoral. And I would bring to the court's notice that great maxim which is the cornerstone of British justice and jury's prudence:

The Law is not Concerned with Trayfulls.

Frank Muir

Where there's a will, there's a way

G. Herbert (1640)
'Outlandish Proverbs'

When it finally became apparent that the entertainment
business was the only career for which I was suited - and
that's quoting my Latin Master more or less exactly - I
went to a large cinema in Leicester Square and pleaded
with them to take me on, in any capacity, however menial.
The Manager said, "The only vacancy I've got is for an Ice
Cream Girl."

"Try me," I said.

I can't say I enjoyed the experience. The shoulder-straps
of those trays are calibrated for feminine sizes, which
meant I had to wear the tray itself so high on my chest, I
kept getting the orange-drink straws up my nostril. So I
was fairly relieved when the Manager told me I was to be
moved to another post.

"You wanted to start at the very bottom rung of the
ladder?" he asked. I nodded. He pointed towards
something propped up against the cinema canopy.
"There's the ladder."

The new job was rather grandly titled 'Head of Display'.
All it really entailed was climbing up the ladder and
affixing, high on the front wall of the cinema, those four-
foot-tall metal letters which spell out the name of the film
on that week.

I can't say it was a glamorous task. In a high wind, it was often dicey and - artistically - it was something less than fulfilling. Unlike a painter or a sculptor, I was in no position to step back and survey my finished work. This led, in the first few weeks, to certain errors of judgment, among which I can remember WEST SIDE SORTY; THE SNOUD OF MUSIC and SANE CONNERY IN GLOD-FINGER.

Nevertheless, the work did make me feel that little bit nearer to the great throbbing heart of show business. If it were not for me, I used to think, as I surveyed the entertainment-hungry crowds milling around Leicester Square, those people would have to make guesses at what we're showing tonight.

But it is only the moment of emergency which really transforms us into troupers. My moment came when the telephone rang at three o'clock one morning. It was the Manager. "I just passed the cinema on my way home from a Ban The Pill meeting," he said. "Your Y has dropped off."

Fuddled with sleep as I was, I immediately comprehended the urgency of his concern. The film we were showing that week was *My Fair Lady*. Although the new liberalisation of attitudes had begun to emerge and Gay Power was already nascent, it was still not yet on for a Leicester Square first-run house to appear to be exhibiting a film called MY FAIR LAD.

When my hastily-summoned taxi reached the cinema, I found the letter Y lying, twisted and splintered, on the pavement. Obviously, it was ruined beyond repair. I hastened to the store-room where the spare letters were kept. There was no spare Y!

Perhaps I can construct one, I thought. Attention was already beginning to be paid to John Schlesinger, Ken Russell and Sam Peckinpah, so we had no shortage of Xs in stock. Perhaps I could take an X and change it into a Y by just sawing off the, as it were, south-east leg?

No luck. I did it all right, but it wouldn't stay up on the

wall. What to do? Where, in London, at four o'clock in the morning, can one lay hands on a four-foot-tall letter Y?

Well, if necessity is the mother of invention, there are times when it is also the mother-in-law. In other words, it can occasionally spur one to the kind of expedient which one would rather not think oneself capable of.

In my case, theft. From the cinema on the opposite side of Leicester Square, which was showing a film whose title contained the letter I wanted. As, at that time of the morning, people get up to all sorts of strange things in the West End, nobody even paused to stare when I shinned up the facia of that cinema and removed its enormous Y.

The only nasty moment came when I was carrying it across Coventry Street. A policeman stopped me - "Excuse me, sir. What might you be doing walking along at 4.30 a.m. carrying a four-foot letter Y?"

Fortunately, I kept my presence of mind, or cool, as it was only just beginning to be called. "This is not a letter Y, officer," I said. "I am an itinerant water-diviner. My preference happens to be for the larger-sized twig.

He even touched his helmet to me as he went on his way. By 5 a.m., the fair name of *My Fair Lady* was restored. True, the cinema opposite, which had been packing them in with a magnificent John Huston classic starring Gregory Peck and Orson Welles, now appeared to be showing a film called MOB DICK. But that's, as I felt myself entitled to say for the very first time, show business.

I've had warm feelings towards the screen version of Herman Melville's great allegorical novel ever since. Indeed, I recommend that any other aspiring Head of Display who ever finds himself in a similar predicament to mine seek around for a cinema showing it. You'll find what I found:

Where there's a whale, there's a Y.

My love is like a red, red rose

Robert Burns

Frank

Are you there Jimmy Young? You of the cheerful chatter
and the gramophone records and the recipe of the day? I
have been a staunch listener this many a year, Jimmy
Young, and I have just tried out one of your recipes so I
thought perhaps you might like to know how it turned
out.

I did everything exactly as you said, picking up pad and
pencil exactly when you told me to - I had to steer with my
teeth - and I obeyed the recipe to the letter.

You do an awful lot of recipes, usually for strange
delights like Savoury Baked-bean Meringues or Pilchard
Tartlets, so you probably don't remember mine offhand -
but it was for a Farmyard Cottage Loaf. Good, old-
fashioned home-made bread.

You began by asking me to grab hold of two pounds of
'plain' flour. You kept repeating that it must be 'plain'
flour but you didn't spell the word 'plain'. Well, Jim, I live
quite near the airport so I dropped in on the way home. Do
you know something? They don't bake on planes. Those
ice-cold sandwiches they hand round are not made on
board; the bread is baked on the ground. So I bought some
flour which the grocer said was 'self-raising'; it seemed the
next best thing.

Then you said "take a pint of water". Bit of a problem there because the bathroom scales only work in stones and pounds. But I found a quart bottle, took this round to the pub and asked the barman to put a pint of draught in it. Once home I got a milk bottle of water and measured how much water I had to add to the beer to fill the bottle. I then emptied the bottle and poured in this same, measured, amount of water. The empty space in the bottle now represented exactly one pint. All I had to do then was fill the bottle and measure how much water it took and I had my pint. As a point of interest, Jim, a pint is roughly the amount contained in a small milk bottle.

Next you said salt - a pinch. No problem; the kitchen window next door was open.

Then came yeast - a lump the size of a walnut - which you said could be obtained from any Baker. I tooled straight round to my nearest Baker, Ernie Baker who mends bicycles, but he'd never heard of the stuff. Luckily I managed to pick up a knob from the cakeshop. It's a sort of yellow dough, Jim, and it stinks.

You then told me to put the flour, yeast, salt and water into a bowl, which I did. You then said that for twenty minutes it had to be kneaded. That was a tricky business, Jim, and I have a couple of hints which you might give your listeners if you repeat this recipe some time in the future. When kneading it is advisable to roll the trousers up first. If you forget to do this and you can't get the dough off with hot water or petrol quite a good tip is to burn the trousers. I found the most practical way of kneading was to divide the dough into two large bowls, put these on the floor and use one knee to each bowl, hanging on to the edge of the kitchen table for balance. Another advantage to this method is that if, as happened to me, the vicar calls in the middle of the process, you can make your way slowly to the front door, Toulouse-Lautrec style, without interrupting the process.

Your next instruction, Jim, was to find a warm place, about 80 degrees Fahrenheit, and put the bowl in to prove it. I found a nice warm spot under the dog and put the bowl in but it didn't prove anything to me. Could have been 20 degrees or 100 degrees, Jim. So I took the bowl out again.

Next I had to grease my baking tin. Now that was something I did know a little about. Out to the garage for the grease-gun. Pump-pump. Done.

Finally you told me to put the dough into the greased tin, press it down well, and bake it in a low oven for four hours. Oh, Jim, that was a tricky one to be faced with right at the end of the recipe. You see, our stove is a pretty old one and it is up on cast-iron legs; the oven is at least eight inches off the ground. But - you wanted a low oven so a low oven you had to have. It took me about twenty minutes to hacksaw off each leg, but I managed it, and in went my bread.

I will be frank with you, Jim, and confess that when I took my loaf out four hours later I was disappointed. It did not even look like a loaf. It was sort of black and blistery and it sat very low in the tin. Nor did it smell like a loaf. It smelt like an Italian garage on a hot day. And I couldn't get it out of the tin. I remember you saying to pass a knife round the edge and shake it out but the knife wouldn't go in. Eventually I drilled a hole in the crust of the loaf, inserted the end of a crowbar and, using the edge of the tin as a fulcrum, threw all my weight on the other end with the object of prising the loaf out. It sort of worked. There was a splintering noise, the crust gave way and I was flat on my back. There was no sign of the interior of the loaf.

I found the interior of the loaf the following morning. On the ceiling. A great lump of semi-cooked, rancid dough had hit the ceiling, started to droop, and then congealed into a cross between a gargoyle and one of those conical plaster ceiling-fittings which electric lights used to hang from.

Far be it from me to criticise, Jim, but are you sure that your recipes aren't a wee bit complicated? I happen to be a handy, practical sort of chap, but many of your listeners are women, Jim, and how some of them would have coped . . .

Well, you said at the end of the recipe that you would like to hear how our bread has turned out so I am only too happy to oblige:

My loaf is like a weird, weird rose.

Prevention is better than cure

Thomas Fuller
'The Histories of the Worthies of England'

Until recently, my knowledge of Herbert Tozer, last of the literalists, was confined to a couple of indignant messages from him. "Kindly refrain from saying 'best foot forward'," he wrote after I had used the phrase in a broadcast. "No one has more than two feet. In future, please amend to 'better foot forward'." Similarly, after I'd uttered publicly the proverb "Still waters run deep", I received a telegram from him - "If waters are still how can they run at all question mark."

Impressed, I showed these admonitions to Sir Jack Longland, our Chairman on that last infirmity of noble minds, the 'My Word!' quiz programme. To my surprise, Jack coloured up like a girl. Then, after some hesitation, he admitted acquaintanceship with Tozer. "It was exactly that trick of literalism," he said "which helped Herbert work his ticket out of the Army."

It was an odd story. Tozer, a National Service conscript, had only been in Catterick Camp two days when he came to the conclusion that the Army was no kind of life for his kind of man. But how to persuade them to sever the connection? He fell back upon literalism.

When, the following morning on the parade-ground, the Sergeant Major instructed his squad to stand at ease,

Herbert left the parade-ground and went absent without leave. They picked him up a week later in a South of England town. On being brought before his C.O., Herbert claimed firmly that he had only been obeying orders. "I was told, sir, that a good soldier always obeys the last order given."

"Your last order, Tozer," the C.O. said coldly, "was to stand at ease."

"With respect, sir, that was not what the Sergeant Major said. If, sir, you would request the Sergeant Major to repeat the order exactly as he uttered it, sir?"

The C.O., a just man, nodded to the Sergeant Major. The S.M. cleared his throat obediently. Then, in traditional manner, he bellowed - "Squa-hod . . . Squad, stand at . . . *hayes*!"

"Exactly, sir. And Hayes is a small town in Middlesex, not far from London Airport. That was where I proceeded to go and stand, sir. As I received no orders rescinding that instruction, sir, I have been standing there these past seven days."

They had no alternative but to acquit and release him. The Army is possibly the last bastion of literalism, particularly with respect to what it calls 'words of command'.

It was this sensitivity that Herbert continued to exploit. Ordered, a couple of days later, to 'Quick March!', he again left the parade-ground. This time he secreted himself within a large ammunition box, inside which he had taken the precaution of boring air-holes and storing ample provisions.

It was five days before they found him. Brought before the C.O., he again requested that the N.C.O. responsible for the quick-march order repeat the word of command. Grimly the C.O. motioned the N.C.O. so to do. "Squa-hod," bellowed the Drill Sergeant. "Squad, quick . . . *hutch*!"

"The verb 'hutch' is a sixteenth-century word," explained Herbert. "It means 'to lay up in a hutch or chest'. And the word 'chest' is defined as 'a large box of strong construction' - an adequate description, I would venture to say, sir, of the container to which I proceeded. And, *en passant,* sir, may I make a suggestion regarding the use of the word 'quick'. It is an adjective, sir. The more correct qualifier would be 'quickly' . . . 'quickly hutch!' ''

The C.O. had little bits of spit showing at the corners of his mouth but, stickler that he was for the niceties, he motioned to Prisoners' Escort to march Herbert away. It was when Herbert appeared before him the very next day, this time following an unconventional response to the command "Eyes Right!", that a despatch-rider was sent to purchase a copy of *The Shorter Oxford English Dictionary*. The command to eyes-right had, as is the Army way, been vouchsafed in the form of "Eyes . . . *hight*!" - whereupon Herbert had smartly proceeded to pull a box of mascara from his battle-dress and daub it profusely upon his eyelashes and eyelids. To the C.O.'s chagrin, the *Shorter Oxford* unequivocally confirmed that 'hight' means 'to embellish or ornament'. (Early M.E., huihten, of doubtful origin, 1633.)

The decisive battle was fought, appropriately, at Herbert Tozer's Passing Out parade. On the very first word of command - the order to come to attention - Herbert marched himself away. This time, however, he was immediately intercepted by the waiting Military Police who had been set to observe his every movement.

On the C.O.'s desk, next to his latest amended copy of Q.R.s - Queen's Regulations, for the non-military - lay the by now well-thumbed *Shorter Oxford*. "All that happened," snarled the C.O., "was that the parade was called to attention. Those were the only words of command given."

"But may I remind you of the manner of their utterance, sir?" Herbert said. "We were told 'Parade . . . *shun*!' The verb 'shun', sir - and do, by all means, look it up - the verb 'shun' means 'avoid, eschew or seek safety by concealment from'. Which I did, sir.''

"And over-reached yourself, Tozer," the C.O. said. "Look, lad." The dictionary flipped open immediately to the correct page, for a book-mark had already been inserted there. "The verb 'shun' can only be used *transitively*. In other words, for it to have the meaning you gave it, there has to be an *object* after it; as in 'shun drink', or 'shun intellectuals'. Without the 'object', its only possible definition is 'Diminutive of stand to attention'. Which you didn't do, cockychops." The C.O. turned to the Adjutant. "Well done, Simon. Think we've got grounds for a court-martial?"

"If you want my opinion, sir," the Adjutant said, "we've got grounds for a firing-squad. Just to make sure, though, I'll send the papers off to the Education Officer, together with a copy of the appropriate Q.R. regarding punishments for desertion."

"In that case, sir," Herbert said, "may I submit a defence-brief to him? Quoting some further references anent the disputed definition?"

"Submit all the anent you wish," said the C.O., who was not without style.

You can't help feeling sorry for the man. What he had forgotten was that no literalist relies on the *Shorter Oxford*. Herbert's brief was based firmly on the thirteen-volume *Oxford*. There, with massive authority, is printed an alternative use of 'shun' - as an *intransitive* verb. Its meaning is 'Move away, go aside, fly'.

Herbert was honourably discharged from the Army within two weeks. The other factor which the C.O. had forgotten was that the Div. Educational Officer was Brigadier J. Longland. Jack's judgment on the relative merits of Herbert's argument as against the Army's was characteristically cogent:

"Brief on 'shun' is better than Q.R."

If winter comes, can spring be far behind?

Percy Bysshe Shelley
'Ode to the West Wind'

Frank

A year or so ago I had occasion to go to Moscow (a cool sentence which tells nothing of the panic, soul-searching, worry and frantic organising which actually took place prior to embarkation). It fell to me, a thrusting, youngish television executive, to see a Russian about a play.

The time of the year was February, and Moscow in February, according to a vodka-pickled ex-foreign correspondent I happened to meet on a 14A bus, is cold enough to freeze the wheels off a brass cannon. So off I went to Moss Bros. and hired myself a fur hat with flaps, galoshes, ski gloves, and an enormous fur-lined overcoat. I held a dress parade when I reached home and my wife said that I looked like a cross between a used flue-brush and a pregnant yeti. Happily my wife was coming with me and I was able to point out that, dressed for the Steppes, she looked like a fur-bearing pear. But at least we reckoned that we would be warm; poor trusting innocents that we were.

I never did like flying and when we arrived at London Airport I had the familiar sensation of disquiet; as though a cold potato had lodged half-way down my gullet.

We arrived in comfortable time, as is our custom; that is to say, two hours before we needed to. Our nerves were not helped by the broadcast announcements. Moscow is a peculiarly upsetting place to be bound for because almost all the half-heard announcements seemed to refer to it: "Last call for flight 724. All passengers mus' go to . . .'' "All passengers for BOAC mus' go . . .'

A further disagreeable factor was the temperature in the Departure Lounge. Reading outwards from my long woollen combs, I was wearing about eight inches of heavy insulation. After five minutes I was sweating like a carthorse.

But we arrived in Moscow safely and perhaps I can pass on a few tips and wrinkles to others preparing a similar expedition.

If you are approached on the tarmac by a photographer who asks you to stand at the top of the aircraft ladder, wave happily, and then step backwards into the aircraft, do benefit from my experience and first make sure that there is an aircraft backed onto the ladder.

Do not have a comeover when you land and find that you are at a place called 'Mockba' and scream that you've been hijacked and try to shut yourself in the loo and have to be given brandy by your wife; 'Mockba' is the way the Russians spell Moscow.

Don't expect too much from Russian plumbing. All Russian lavatory cisterns are made by the same firm and none of them works. Or rather, they overwork. Instead of the water gushing forth on demand, building up again, and then stopping, due to a small design deficiency there is no build-up and no gush on demand, just a steady, noisy trickle of water through the works night and day. So what you do is this. You take the porcelain lid off with your right hand and feel down in the water with your left hand. Somewhere at the bottom there is a rubber seating-valve thing. Press this firmly down and the trickle ceases.

Note to the above: A little way up Gorki Prospect, on the left, is a small jeweller's shop which specialises in drying out wrist-watches.

The steward on the aircraft told me always to wear my

fur hat and always to wear it with the flaps down and the strings tied firmly under my chin, and I think this was very good advice. The only thing is that fur hats are very bulky things and at first I kept rolling out of bed. This can be avoided by stacking a couple of bricks on the pillow either side of the head.

I have left the Golden Tip until last, because it is very important and I had to find it out for myself.

There is a fallacy in the system of clothing you are advised to wear to combat the Russian winter. When you are standing erect the clothing is warm enough; but when you are walking, or bending down . . .

All fur-lined overcoats have a slit up the back. All jackets have a slit up the back. All winter long-johns have a slit up the back. When you bend down in Red Square there is nothing between your vitals and the east wind of Siberia but the seam in your trousers - virtually a dotted line. Your rear portion is almost totally unprotected; a sitting target for frostbite.

I gave the problem considerable thought and came up with a practical answer. You take *two* fur hats with you to Moscow. Each morning, before dressing, in the privacy of your own bedroom, you arrange two basins on two chairs. In basin A you stir a mixture of flour and water until it reaches the consistency of cream. You then take a pair of scissors and your second fur hat and snip off enough fur to fill basin B. Lowering your pyjama trousers (or raising your nightdress, as appropriate) you sit in basin A. You then walk about a bit until tacky and sit in basin B. A further turn round the room to dry off and you are fully protected for twenty-four hours against the iciest wind blowing round the Urals.

But, you are probably saying, the flaps on my long winter underwear always stays shut; and anyway, I won't be bending down.

I say, don't take chances. They can spring open with the ordinary movements of walking. So:

If winter combs can spring - befur behind.

A crown is no cure for the headache

Benjamin Franklin
'Poor Richard's Almanack'

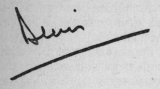

My grandmother was a great one for axioms. Her favourite was, 'The unexpected doesn't always happen but when it does it generally happens when you're least expecting it.' As with everything else about my little smiling Granny, that axiom is sagacious, perceptive and, when you get right to the core of the situation, absolutely no help at all.

If you require some elaboration of that touch of bitterness, stay with me. We'll go back to the time when I was seventeen years old.

When I was seventeen, it was a very good year for small-town girls. Mainly because not one of them would have anything to do with me. This was due to the appearance I presented. At that age I was all wrists and ankles. Six foot three, a neck like Nat Jackley's, so gangling and painfully skinny that, in repose, I looked like a pair of discarded braces.

Such a configuration made me achingly shy of girls. In fact, at the time of which I speak, I still hadn't kissed any female who was not either a blood-relation or four-legged.

Then one day, a Tuesday afternoon, while Jan Berenska belted out his concert arrangement of 'Little Curly Head Upon A High Chair' direct from the Pump Room, Leamington Spa, my Mum came into my bedroom. "Mrs

Forbush is coming to tea," she said. "And she's bringing her daughter with her. You two can play together while we talk."

The news did not stir me. Although I'd never seen the daughter, I had seen Mrs Forbush. About as sexy as the General Council of the TUC. So I just grunted and continued cutting out the advertisements for half-slips in *The Draper's Record*. An hour later, the door opened again and my mother pushed Lila in.

Lila. Thinking back on her, even across this arch of decades, my marrow-bone still melts. A raven-eyed, black-haired shimmer of wet-lipped ripeness. Just turned sixteen, and wearing those shiny artificial-silk stockings with the overstated seam.

"Well," my Mum said as she left us, "play nicely." I remained inert, just gazing at Lila. Never, in the whole of my life-span, had I ever gazed on anything so utterly - *tangible*.

She scanned me the way a decorator does a house when you've asked for an estimate to do the outside. I said, "Would you like to look through my Meccano catalogues?"

She shook her head. The movement rippled right the way down! I could hear my own breathing. "Tell you what," she said, in a light clear voice, "let's kiss."

It was just the one kiss. What must be said about it, though, is that it lasted twenty-three minutes. Moreover, the embouchure which Lila employed can most nearly be conveyed by the phrase 'as though eating an over-ripe pear'. My Chilprufe vest ran up my back like a window-blind.

Immediately after it, we were called downstairs for tea and Lyons Snow Cake, so that's all there ever was between Lila Forbush and me. She showed no inclination to go upstairs again after tea, spent the rest of the afternoon chatting to my Mum and Mrs Forbush, without even glancing in my direction. I sensed that she'd found me to be what educational circles now describe as an under-achiever.

Episode closed. But where does an experience like that, with a Lila like that, leave a man for the rest of his life? I am in a position to tell you. Ever afterwards, she becomes the measure against which every other woman fails. Then, as he moves towards middle-age - "If only," he keeps finding himself thinking. "If only we could play it again Sam. With me as I am now - but Lila as she was then!"

Impossible? Well, hold your horses. Cut to thirty years later. This month, in fact. Two weeks ago, if you want it to the day, at a friend's cocktail-party in the King's Road. He'd just taken over a disused telephone-box and opened it as a boutique. There I was, milling with the fashionable throng, when - suddenly, right in front of me, across a crowded room - ! Unmistakable. Those raven-eyes, the black hair, those pouting wet lips! It had happened! Life had managed to work me its jackpot - a second chance!

I bounded across that room like an antelope. Trying to control my voice, "My dear," I said. "Please don't be startled, I'm not accosting you. It's just that, are you - oh, you must be, I can see it in every feature - are you Lila Forbush's daughter?"

The light, clear tone which answered me erased three decades as though they had never been. "Up your kilt, squire."

"No, please," I said. "Don't turn away, I mean no offence."

"Well you're giving it, aren't you?

"Why?"

"I'm Lila Forbush's son."

I refer you back to my grandmother's axiom. Also, and more importantly, to that assertion that axioms offer the thinking man everything except consolation.

Or, as Ben Franklin used to walk around America snarling:

"A gran is no cure for the heartache."

A rose-red city - 'half as old as time'

Rev. John William Burgon
'Petra'

Frank

I have been near tears many times in my crowded life but I
can only recall having actually wept but twice - once when I
rounded a bend of the road in Corsica and the unbelievable
beauty of the rock formations known as Les Calanches
were bathed in the warm, rosy glow of the late afternoon
sunshine, and once when a horse trod on my foot.

But I was near tears today, when the post brought me a
birthday card from a dear old lady in the village. She was
in hospital - she had twisted her ankle water-skiing in
Hendon - and had taken the trouble to make me a birthday
card with her own hands. Just a folded piece of simple
paper, with a pressed flower pasted on the front, and a
simple legend within: 'Happy Birthday. With all the money
you're making, how about sending an old lady a gallon of
gin. Mrs Tobler.'

Oh it wasn't the words, simple and sincere though they
were. It was something about the faded flower pasted on
the front. And the name Mrs Tobler. Where had I seen that
flower before?

Later on that morning, as I was cleaning my spectacles,
everything became clear.

It was twelve years ago, give or take a day. And it was to
do with my children. Jamie was then six feet tall, with an

engaging smile and a lot of blonde hair. He was eight. A quiet lad, for the past few months he had been spending most of his spare time industriously loosening and removing his teeth in order to save up sixpences thereby obtained to buy a chemistry set to make ice cream. My daughter Sally was six; gentle, beautiful and practically toothless because Jamie was helping to loosen her teeth in return for half her sixpences.

The children had a part of the garden for their very own, to make of it what they would. Jamie had made a mine of his. He was down about eight feet, prospecting for old clay pipes, coal, Roman coins, mud; anything on which he could make an honest buck.

Sal's patch was quite different. She loved colour, and simple things, and beauty. Her little square was neatly raked and levelled and she had put little labels where she had planted things. She had planted a number of things. There was a sandal. It showed no signs of growing but nor did it deteriorate; it stuck out of the ground and sort of retained its status quo. There was one asparagus which had roared up to a height of four feet and waved in the breeze like a ghostly, emaciated Christmas tree. A packet of frozen peas. In their packet. And a rose bush. Sal was very, very attached indeed to her rose bush. She had cut a clipping on a country walk and planted it and it made a brave patch of colour - mostly brown and green - but there was one small, red flower. Sal had called it *Red Setter*. Because it was a dog-rose.

Now we had an actor staying with us at the time named Arthur Howard. A very nice actor indeed. The sort of actor who when you say to somebody "We've got Arthur Howard staying with us" they say "Oh, ARTHUR! How IS he?" But Arthur was not a gardener. Actor, yes. Gardener, no. *The Tempest* - fine. The compost - not a clue.

That afternoon we had to go out on a charity walk - well a sort of charity walk; my wife was breaking in a new pair of boots for the parish priest - and Arthur could not

106

come with us because he had caught his ear in the egg whisk. It was one of those hand-held ones like a bow-legged ballet dancer doing an entrechat and, thinking two of the tines were touching, he whirred it round and put his ear to it . . .

So we left Arthur to look after the estate.

When we arrived back it seems that a woman - a Mrs Tizer, or Tusser, Arthur couldn't be sure - had arrived at the back door and asked whether she could buy some of my wife's herbs. My wife had her little herb garden right next to the children's patch.

Ever eager to oblige, Arthur had pulled up handfuls of this and that and sold them to the woman for a shilling.

"What did you give her?" asked my wife, a little puzzled.

"Well," said Arthur, "there was rosemary, chives, tarragon, and - oh yes - thyme!"

"Are you sure?" asked my wife "I don't remember planting thyme."

The next thing there was a tremendous cry and Sally hurtled into the scene, tears streaming down her face. "My rose has gone!" she sobbed. "Somebody has stolen my lovely rose!"

And gone it had. Her single little dog-rose had vanished from the face of the earth, it seemed for ever.

But this morning it returned. Dried, pressed, and stuck to my birthday card from the old lady; twelve years later.

So a few minutes ago, when Sally looked at the card in my hand in a rather puzzled way and said "What is that flower? It seems - sort of - familiar," who can begrudge me a vagrant tear as I answered, "It is a rose, dearest . . .

"A rose, *Red Setter*, Arthur sold as thyme."

More matter with less art

William Shakespeare
'Hamlet'

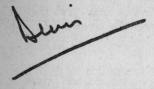

Ever see a Burt Lancaster war-film called *The Train?* A dull title, but an interesting premise - a group of French civilians who risk their lives smuggling certain masterpieces of French art out of the occupied zone, so that the noble culture of La Belle France can continue to enrich the spirit of the Free World. The question the film posed was this: is the preservation of any work of art, however great, worth the sacrifice of any human life, however humble?

I found myself facing the same philosophical dilemma when my small nephew got his head jammed in the hole of a Henry Moore statue. It was during a class outing to the Tate Gallery and young Arthur had paused in front of Moore's *The Mother*. What the teacher should have remembered was that, the previous week, the same class had been on a day-trip to Brighton. There, on the Palace Pier, Arthur had posed for a comic photograph in one of those 'fat lady' cut-outs with a hole at the neck for you to stick your own face through.

To the mind of a twelve-year-old, the association of ideas must have been irresistible. Even the Gallery authorities admitted that it was a justifiable impulse, not to say endearing. It only began to take on dimensions when they found Arthur couldn't get his head out of the statue again.

"We've tried everything," the Curator said when he visited me that evening. "Cutting his hair, greasing his ears . . ." He gestured helplessly.

My own knowledge of modern sculpture can be evaluated from the fact that I once put down £75 deposit on a Giacometti under the impression it was an Italian sports car. So I cannot say I really appreciated the Curator's agitation. Not even when he said, "It looks as though the only way we'll ever extricate your nephew is by smashing that statue to pieces."

"Fair enough," I said. "Want the lend of a big hammer?"

He twitched. "Henry Moore's *The Mother*," he said, "is one of this country's finest cultural treasures."

"I see," I said. "Well, that's more than anyone could say about Arthur. Judging from his school reports, that hole is about the only 'O' he'll ever get through."

The Curator drew a shaky breath. "Look here. Are we to demolish a masterwork just because of one idiot schoolboy?"

I stared at him. There was a cold glitter in his eye. "I want you, as his uncle, to persuade his parents to let him . . . stay there."

"Stone me," I said.

"We'll do everything that can be done to ensure that he leads as normal a life as is possible under the circumstances. The Arts Council has already promised a special grant."

"It's still not much of a future for the lad, is it," I said. "Oh, may be all right for the time being, but what about when he's a bit older? Girls? Marriage? You'd have your work cut out then, wouldn't you? Oh, I suppose he could manage some kind of married life, not the easiest, but what about if he has children? I mean, think of things like Speech Day? Couldn't very well turn up with a statue round his neck, could he, you know how kids are about their parents looking conspicuous."

"It's the boy," said the Curator, "or the statue."

Well, it was one of your metaphysical posers. 'Art versus Life'. Oh, I know your Jonathan Millers and your Dr Bronowskis can bat a topic like that up an down for hours, but it was outside my range. Deepest I've ever been on a chat-show is Are Blood Sports Cruel. So I said "Mind if I go and have a look at Arthur?"

The Tate Gallery at midnight can never be what a person would call groovy. That night, however, the sight of that enormous statue with a schoolboy's head in the middle . . . macabre. I said to the Curator, "You could at least have altered the label. Called it *Mother And Child*."

Young Art, I must say, was in excellent spirits, considering. "Hallo, uncle," he said. "Got me head stuck."

There was something in his tone I recognised. "Arthur," I said, "you're enjoying this."

He smiled. "Got 'em all at it, haven't I."

I realised what was needed. "Arthur," I said, "when your parents had the wall removed between your lounge and your dining-room, do you remember what they called that?"

"Yes," he said. "Knocking-through."

I brought the big hammer out of my pocket. "That's the phrase I was looking for."

In ten seconds he was standing by my side. "Can we stop for a kebab on the way home?"

It was, I think, the magazine called *Studio International* which made use of the *Hamlet* quotation. They displayed two photographs - one showing the scene before Arthur was extricated, the other showing the scene afterwards. The 'before' one was captioned, 'Henry Moore's *The Mother* With Arthur Inside'. On the photo of the empty statue, the caption read:

'Moore *Mater* With Less Art'

Stand a little less between me and the sun

Diogenes to Alexander, when the latter asked if there was anything he could do for him.

Frank

I was very interested to read in *The Times* the other day that Claude Monet's painting, *Girl walking by the river near St Cloud,* had been sold at Sotheby's for £1,000,000,000. The buyer was an American from Texas who wanted it very much to make into a drinks tray. I wasn't able to read the buyer's name because it was just below the chips and the paper had gone transparent.

I suppose it went for what these days is a largish sum because it is such an important painting; the first painting in which the great Impressionist had included a human figure. Just what induced him to break the habit of a lifetime and shove in a girl I am now able to divulge.

Monet started to paint his picture - the one he put the figure in - on the morning before the first Impressionist exhibition. This took place in Paris, in 1874, in the studio of the photographer Nader - 35 Boulevard des Capucines, first door on the left, over the chemist's shop.

That morning all the young painters met in a café - the Café Guerbois, second on the right past the horsemeat shop - and a very excited batch of poor young painters they were, to be sure, laughing and shouting and ordering drinks.

There was Toulouse-Lautrec; he was on shorts. There

111

was the nervous, brooding young Vincent Van Gogh, who tossed back his drink and strode off ("Young Vincent is so restless," murmured Monet, "ear today - gone tomorrow"). There was Sisley, Fantin-Latour, all drinking down litres of cheap beer. Only Cézanne was conspicuous by his absinthe.

But the figure of Claude Monet sat apart from the others, moodily stirring his coffee with a used tube of Chrome Yellow, and not joining in the general fun of pouring beer over each other and throwing bread at the waiter.

"What's up, Claude, *mon vieux*?" cried Alfred Sisley, flinging himself bestride the chair next to Monet and wincing a moment with agony.

"Well, you've done it all wrong, lads," replied Monet. "All you've painted is women. Dozens and dozens of plump birds. The public doesn't want plump birds - they're a drug on the market. I doubt if you can flog another painting of a plump bird even if you give trading stamps."

"But," stuttered Sisley, adjusting his chair, "have you seen Renoir's study of the girl bathing by the river? Beautiful . . . meaningful . . ."

"Like a mauve sea-cow sitting on wet grass, old son. He'll be trundling that home on the old pram tonight, mark my words."

"But . . . have you seen Degas' pastel of the naked woman bending over a bowl of water?"

"A flash in the pan, squire. He'll get ten francs for it, top weight, frame thrown in. No, laddie, it's the old pastoral scene they want these days; the old sun through the trees and glinting off the old water and not a body in sight. So good luck with the exhibish - I'm off to dash off a quickie along the banks of the Seine; there's a nice bend near St Cloud where the water's a dark brown colour; I've got rather a lot of brown left over from that thing I did of Rouen Cathedral . . . *allez-au'voir!*" And he was gone.

And so, on the evening of the 15 April, 1874, the young Impressionists startled Paris with their first exhibition. In no time at all the little salon was filled to bursting point with the cream of Paris.

Emile Zola was there with his lovely wife, Gorgon. The poet Baudelaire rushed about all over the place, uttering little cries and simply reeking of 'Fleurs du Mal'.

The British Ambassador, Lord Macbeth, was there with his lady wife. Lady Macbeth was visibly startled at the painting of the woman bending over the bowl and cried "Is that a Degas I see before me?"

George Sand, the eminent lady novelist, swept in like a ship in full sail with her usual two admirers in attendance; a Chopin to starboard and a Liszt to port.

Probably the most excited person present was the Spanish consul, who stood in front of Renoir's picture of the large nude lady sitting on the turf crooning *"Gracias!* Oh, *gracias!"*

In one hour and ten minutes every picture had been sold. Not for thirty or forty francs, as the poor young artists had hoped, but for a hundred francs and more.

The Spanish consul paid two hundred francs for Renoir's nude and insisted on taking it with him. He cried, "I just cannot leave her behind alone!"

As the evening light began to fade, Renoir took a cab to St Cloud to find his old friend Claude and tell him the good news. He soon found him, on a corner of the Seine, dabbing away at the brown bits of his picture.

"Claude!" he shouted, "Claude, you must paint women! Put one in your picture now. This instant! We have all sold every one of our figure pictures!"

"And how much did you get for your purple sea-cow, matey, eh? Five francs? Ten?

In answer, Renoir counted out his two hundred francs.

"Good grief!" said Claude, "Deux song frong for embongpong?"

He looked down at his painting of the river and the empty riverbank.

"Would you do something for me?" he asked, a strange look coming into his eyes.

"Of course, replied Renoir. "What do you want me to do?"

Claude Monet took up a great brushful of pink paint: "Stand a little lass between me and the Seine."

Dressed in a little brief authority

William Shakespeare
'Measure for Measure'

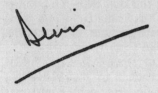

The outpost of Arcadia in which I live is called Golders Green. It features a Mrs Thora Tidmarsh who gives the kind of parties that could count as qualifying heats for the Olympic Yawning Team. At one of them, a piece of paper was pinned on your lapel as you came through the front door. On this paper was written an anagram and you had to promise faithfully you wouldn't help yourself to a drink until you'd worked it out what word the anagram was supposed to be. My anagram was CXLNOIE.

That was eighteen months ago. Last week I met Thora Tidmarsh in the Chinese Take-Away and she said, "I'm having another party next Saturday, you must come. Everyone's got to dress up as a famous quotation."

"Mrs Tidmarsh," I said, "Oh, Mrs Tidmarsh."

"Lexicon. That's the word. Lexicon! CXLNOIE. Look, you won't mind if I rush this a bit from now on, will you, but it's been eighteen months since I tasted alcohol."

When I got home, my wife said, "I'm going as, you'll never guess the quotation, it came to me like Flash, I'm going as, no I won't tell you."

I said, "What are you going as?"

She said, "I'm going to carry a flask of wine and a loaf of bread and a big card with the word OHTU."

I said, "I've got it. I bet I've got it. It's 'OHTU be in England now that - '."

"It's not," she said. "It's 'A flask of wine, a loaf of bread and thou'. OHTU is the anagram."

I said, "But anagrams were only for the last party, this party's it's - oh, you get on with it then."

But every day from then on, she kept exclaiming things like, "You'll never guess what Mrs Thing from 74's going as. She's going to hang a convector heater on her bottom and be 'O that this too, too solid flesh would melt'." Or, "You know the lady who lives at 'Done Rome In'?" (The husband claims to be a descendant of the Visigoths.) "Well, she's embroidering the minicab company's price-rises on her blouse, so as to be 'Earth has not anything to show more fare'."

People can be so creative sometimes, can't they. Me, I just gloomed about for the whole week, brain-racking. Friday night, I still hadn't an idea in my head, so I said, "Listen, why don't I just pitch up at the back door and instead of going in, I'll hang about outside and be 'Come into the garden, Maud'?"

She said, "Where does the Maud bit fit in?"

I said, "You're getting more like your mother every day."

Comes Saturday night, I'm no further on. Away she went with her flask of wine and her Hovis and I said I'd join her a bit later because my mind works better under deadline conditions. After about an hour of sitting with my eyes closed, the hunger pangs struck, so I wandered into the larder ('When did you last see your larder?'?). All I could find were a couple of rather pallid soft roes ('Go, lovely Roes'?), a box of Matzos ('You Matzo been a beautiful baby?'), and - ah now! Wait a minute.

On the bottom shelf there was this bit of cheese. A large slice of Brie that we used for the mousetrap, the mice round N.W.11 being a bit sophisticated.

I took off all my clothes, stripped right down to the skin, smeared myself from head to foot with the Brie cheese, which luckily was fairly ripe, or 'Muir' as the French call it, slipped on my raincoat, then off I trotted to the party.

I was, though I say it myself, a sensation. Mainly, I think, because I went to the wrong house. There were about eight people round the table when I was ushered in, all of them in evening dress like one of those after-dinner mint adverts, and they evinced some consternation.

"Sorry," I said. "Mistake. Thought this was Thora Tidmarsh's place. She's giving a party and I'm a quotation."

"Oh, quite understandable," they said. "Not to worry. Think nothing of it. My hacienda is yours, senor. But," they said, "why are you smothered all over in runny cheese?"

"Ah, that," I said. "Well, it's *Shakespeare,* isn't it?

" 'Dressed in a little Brie for Thora T'."

BOOK TWO

Upon My Word !

'The Light That Failed'

Rudyard Kipling
Title of Story

[signature]

It's fair to say that, even at my most unbuttoned, I am to
the Fun People what Marcel Marceau is to radio. For that
reason, it was perhaps unwise even to have considered
accepting that invitation to Bernice's Housecooling Party.
Bernice, by common agreement of every After Eight
consumer in the Garden Suburb, is more or less a
registered Fun Person. So for me to receive an invite to one
of her celebrations was very akin to breaking through the
Roundhead lines.

For the benefit of those of you who don't live at that
pace either, I should explain that a Housecooling party is
one thrown to mark the *departure* from a house. In
Bernice's case, this was occasioned by the fact that she and
Lionel had finally split up. I say 'finally' because although
divorce had been on the cards for ages, they'd been trying
to make a go of it for the sake of the home movies.

Now, however, the split was official and Bernice was
launching her new status with champagne and the chums
round and I felt no end chuffed at being included among
those cavorting. The only snag was, what should I take
along as a present? What sort of gift is *appropriate* to a
Fun Person? Yes, obviously a Fun *Thing* - but then again,
what's that? I did a tentative wander round our local Gift

121

Boutique, but that's not really an Aladdin's Cave even at the best of times and especially not since it branched out into Suede Cleaning and Sheepskin Renewal.

Contact sunglasses? An electric kettle with a stereo whistle? A musical toilet-roll holder that plays 'Dream The Impossible Dream'? Everything I considered seemed far too *stolid* for a fun-gift. Then, the following Sunday, my eye lighted on an item in the newspaper: a trendy foundry in the Midlands was offering reproduction chastity-belts! Perfect replicas, in cast iron, of the famed mediaeval securi-corps, complete with padlock and key.

When I presented one to Bernice, I must say its reception proved all I could have hoped for. "Oh, what a Fun Thing!" she ejaculated. "Do look everybody, oh do look!" She's a large lady, Bernice, and as she never wears undergarments, when she walks everything seems to move more than her feet do. Right now, her motion was that of a blancmange in a railway dining-car. "Isn't it a hoot!" she shouted. "Oh, Giorgio, do come and look."

Giorgio turned out to be an Italian water-skiing instructor she'd recently imported from Portofino. About seven-foot tall, sun-tanned, muscles even unto the eyebrows, and didn't speak one word of English. "Isn't it absolutely darling?" she yelled, waving the belt in front of him. "Chastitia Belta!" He nodded uncomprehendingly and grinned, exposing teeth you could read small print by.

"Bags you try it on," shouted the man who manages the Driving School, an ex-major with gin leaking out of his ears. "Go on, Bernice, put it on!"

"Oh I must, I must! Give me just five mins."

While she was upstairs, I was man of the moment. Everybody crowded round me and said what a brilliant idea, what really fun-thinking, how absolutely knockout, and you really must come round to our pad for fondue. And when Bernice came down again, "It fits as if it was made for me," she squealed. "Absolutely superb, darling."

Then, while everybody was uttering cheers and upping their glasses to me, she waved her hands in the air. "A moment's quiet now," she said. "Best of order, please. It's time for Bernice to make the big announcement."

She moved over to Giorgio and leaned back against the brown wall of his chest. "This morning at eleven o'clock, Giorgio and I were married in Hampstead Registry Office. Tonight we're off to Portofino for the honeymoon bit."

A moment's gaping - then whoops and yoicks. Hugging, back-slapping, cries of congratulations from all the males, envy from the females. They poured champagne the way Wimpeys pour concrete and, after someone had put the Marriage Theme from *The Godfather* on the record-player, dancing took place.

So when, an hour or so later, Bernice came quivering up at my side, I was feeling no angst at all. "Just off to change into the going-away gear, darling," she smiled. "Can I have the padlock key?"

"By jove, yes," I chuckled. "Jolly well better have that, I should think, what?" I don't know why I seem to fall into that playing-against-type sort of dialogue in Fun People environments, nerves I suppose, but anyway I reached jovially into my pocket for the small cast-iron key.

It was the first time I ever really comprehended the meaning of that expression 'suddenly taken sober'. As I groped from pocket to pocket, I could *feel* the room cooling. Slowly all conversation died, the record-player was switched off, more and more eyes turned to me as I patted myself, poked, dug, scrabbled, tore. By the time I had every single one of my pocket-linings hanging out, the place was in complete silence. The only sound to be heard came from the TV set next door. It was a commercial; the one about 'all that locked-in goodness'.

"Surely," said somebody finally, "surely they come with a *spare* key."

"Well, no. Not if you think about it," I said. "I mean not for a chastity-belt. A spare key, I mean, it'd sort of defeat the whole . . . '' It was a trailing-off kind of state-ment, because nobody seemed all that interested in pursuing its logic. From upstairs we heard Giorgio burst into sudden song. Having gone up to change into his other tee-shirt, he was cheerfully belting out the Italian version of 'Tonight, tonight, Won't be just any night.'

"Send for the Fire Brigade," said Bernice, her eyes never leaving mine and all that mighty mass at rest.

The first thing the Head Fireman said when he came through the door was "Will I need the extension ladder?" I took him out on to the patio and gave him a complete, if muttered, explanation of the circumstances. He stared at me, "I've got two engines and an appliance out there," he said. "We've halted the traffic up as far as Swiss Cottage."

"An appliance," I said. That's exactly what's needed. Some kind of appliance."

He shouldered the hose and spoke a few dismissive words into a walkie-talkie. As the mighty engines roared into life and started moving away, he said, "Don't you know it's an offence to make unnecessary 999 calls? I'll lend you a six-inch cold file and consider yourself lucky."

Clutching the ugly metal implement he'd pushed into my hand, I said to Bernice, "Let's go up in the bathroom then." When I felt the little stir of air caused by a whole roomful of eyebrows lifting, I quickly added, "I'll wear some kind of blindfold, of course. Whole thing won't take more than a few minutes."

Nor would it have done. Except that Giorgio, sensing his new bride's presence in the bathroom, took it into his head to burst joyously in upon her.

I've tried many times to interpret the scene as it must have presented itself to his eyes. Bearing in mind that he hadn't grasped the function of my gift in the first place, all he registered was this stranger wearing a rubber shower-cap pulled down over his eyes, kneeling in front of Bernice - and creating this *rasping* noise. . . .

Well it's all water under the bridge now and I'm not really complaining. As soon as I was considered well enough to eat solids again, Giorgio even had the generosity to send me a box of fruit jellies. But what's beyond all doubt is this: as far as moving in on the Fun People is concerned. I've blown all chances.

In fact, I doubt if my name is even acknowledged by any of them any more. If I'm ever mentioned at all, it's only by the fun-soubriquet Giorgio used in addressing his jellies - 'Lo zotico que limó'.

Don't bother getting out the Italian dictionary. The translation is etched upon my cortex:

'The Lout That Filed.'

Let us now praise famous men,
and the fathers that begat us

Ecclesiasticus xliv. 1

I answered the front door one evening and there stood a thinnish, faintly familiar figure.

"Yes?" I said.

"It's me!" said the figure. "Nicholas. Nicholas Menon. Husband of Carol. Your vicar."

I peered. "So it is! Come in, old friend!"

I persuaded him to accept a glass of herbal mixture - the juice of juniper berries, distilled, with ice and lemon and not too much tonic - and brought the conversation round to the change in his appearance.

"You used to be thick, Nick," I said, groping for tactful words. "But you've lost a lot of weight. You're now, how can I put it, a slicker vicar. What pared away the pounds? A diet? Dietary biscuits? A cellular wafer?"

"A glandular fever. But herein lies my problem. My clothes are now four sizes too large and I am to officiate at a wedding tomorrow."

"As indeed I know," I answered warmly. "The *Staines and Egham News* is my bible. Sunninghill Parish Church. Morning-suits, marquee among the rhododendrons and the cream of the *Tatler's* photographic staff."

"Even so," he said. "Now, I have found one suit that fits me, a clerical grey number from my student days which was lagging the church boiler, and I have taken it to the cleaners in Virginia Water. They assure me that it will be ready for collection just before I have to set out for the wedding tomorrow.''

"Well, that should do the trick, Nick." I replied. "Wherein lies your problem?''

"The manager of the cleaners has just telephoned to say that his pressing machine has expired in a cloud of steam. My suit will be cleaned, spun in a drum until dry, but, alas, not pressed.''

"Ah!" I said. "So you either officiate tomorrow looking like Stan Laurel wearing Oliver Hardy's suit, or wearing a suit straight out of the spin-dryer, wrinkled like a walnut.''

"There seems no other choice.''

I mixed us another half-litre of herbal comfort.

"Timings?'' I asked.

"Collect suit, 2.30. Drive back to Thorpe Vicarage and change at great speed. Arrive at the church at 2.50. I can just do the journey in 16 minutes - Carol timed me yesterday with the kitchen plunger.''

I am a firm believer in Lateral Thinking in problems like these. So I assumed a Lateral position on the carpet and gave myself up to Thought. After, I suppose, some nine minutes I sat up.

"We will be waiting for you at the cleaners tomorrow with a vehicle," I said, emphasising each word. "You will enter the vehicle, with your suit, and be driven to the church. On the way your suit will be neatly pressed - WHILE IT IS ON YOU!''

His face was a study.

There were all too few hours left for preparation, for racing round to the builder's merchants, the camping equipment shop, the ironmongers, to say nothing of persuading Mr Marshall to lend us his Mobile Green-grocery van.

2.30 the next day saw my wife, son and I, in Mr Marshall's van, waiting outside the cleaners in Virginia

Water. My wife had lit two camping stoves and fixed the rubber tubing to the spouts of the two kettles. Jamie was keeping the engine running for a smooth getaway.

Nicholas emerged, clutching his clean but crumpled suit, and looking, I thought, a shade apprehensive.

Once Nick was in the van, Jamie let in the clutch and proceeded towards Sunninghill. Nick changed into his suit in a secluded corner by the cabbages and on my word of command assumed a prone position on the floor.

Rolling forward the two three-foot lengths of six-inch diameter, salt glaze pottery drainage pipes I deftly slipped them up Nick's legs. There was an awkward moment when his right shoe jammed in the pipe but a blow or two with the starting handle freed the foot and no time was lost. Polly's kettles were then on the boil and, on the word of command, she inserted the rubber tubes up the pipes.

We allowed the steam to play through the pipes for six minutes. I then slid the pipes away from the legs and Nick stood up for the next stage, which consisted of applying bulldog clips so as to form creases in the damp, hot fabric. Eighty of these were clipped on, twenty to each crease, back and front, both legs. As Nick sat on the tailboard of the van, dangling his legs in the airstream to dry off his trousers, we began on the jacket.

First we removed the jacket, replacing it with a heat-proof waistcoat made by my wife from eighteen oven gloves sewn together. Next we dampened the jacket with water from the watering-can Mr Marshall used to freshen up his lettuces. We then replaced the jacket on Nick, and covered the entire surface of the jacket, sleeves as well, in oven-proof aluminium foil. After checking that Nick was completely foiled, I lit my little calor-gas blow torch and began playing it carefully over the foil, keeping it moving, watching for tell-tale puffs of steam which told me that the scheme was working.

At one point Nick seemed to slump.

"Are you all right?" I enquired, anxiously. "Not the old ticker, vicar?"

But it was only some large potatoes which had fallen off a high rack, when Jamie had taken a right-hand bend at speed, and hit Nicholas on the head.

We stripped off the hot foil, held the jacket out of the window to cool it off, and the job was done.

At 2.49 precisely my son pulled up with a jerk outside the gates of Sunninghill church, a rain of assorted choice veg descended upon us, and Nick got out of the van and made his way towards the vestry door, looking smart and neat in his well-pressed suit.

He was still steaming a little here and there but we reckoned that anybody noticing it in church would assume it to be a kind of nimbus.

"Well," said my wife, plucking a brussels sprout from her hair. "Thank goodness that's over."

"Over?" I said, incredulity in my voice. "Over? It hasn't really started yet. We are on our way to our first million with the Muir On-Site Valet Van!"

"You don't really suppose you can make money with this . . . this . . ."

"Consider," I said, my voice rising with boyish enthusiasm. "It'll be the Fourth of June soon. Founder's Day at Eton. Statesmen, judges and millionaires trudging along Eton High Street, suits crumpled after sitting all day in deck-chairs watching cricket. I step out of the van, parked by the kerb. 'Touch up, my lord? Just step inside!' And then there's Henley Regatta. Hundred's of old chaps in little pink caps - Leanderthal Man - watching their sons skulling up an down and wondering how they are going to make the old blazer last through the week. 'Care for a spruce-up before your son wins the race, sir? Polly - put the kettles on!' Thank goodness that Nick started us going."

"What are you trying to say?"

"Let us now press famous men, and the fathers at regattas!"

Discretion is the better part of valour

Proverb

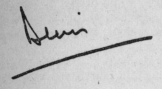

I was watching a blue movie the other night - it wasn't
meant to be that colour, but my TV set hasn't been the
same since I turned it over on its side to watch mre comfortably while lying in bed - and it was one of those
wartime flying stories.

My mind immediately snapped back to that summer of
1941 when I was a Lab. Technician in the Photographic
Unit of an RAF Training Station up in Northern Scotland.
Our task was to teach budding Intelligence Officers how to
'read' Aerial Reconnaissance photographs. (Oh, you
remember what they were - those photos of enemy terrain
which were taken from a great height by our reconnaissance planes.)

My part in this training operation was boring but simple.
Whenever we received an A.R. photo ('Aerial Reconnaissance'; come on now, don't make me have to explain everything), I would inspect it, select an appropriate square of
it, blow that square up into a ten-by-eight glossy, then pass
out several copies of this enlargement among the I.O.s.
They would study their ten-by-eights through magnifying
glasses, then each would take his turn interpreting the
significant topographical features suggested by the photo:
reservoirs, high ground, railway lines, wooded areas, etc.

Got the hang of it now? I hope so, because I now have to explain some of the handicaps under which I worked.

The principal one was that I never *received* any Aerial Reconnaissance photographs. Oh, Reconnaissance Command posted them to me all right, but as they were somewhere down in the Home Counties and the part of Northern Scotland we were in was really excessively Northern, the mail never reached us. Consequently I was obliged to obtain my supply of A.R. photos from whatever alternative sources I could find.

Well, at that time and in that place, there was only one alternative source - elderly back-numbers of the *National Geographic Magazine,* which the Dental Officer kept in his ante-room, presumably because anaesthetics were also in short supply. Several of these contained Aerial Photographs which were quite adequate for my purposes. As they were usually of places like The Great Barrier Reef or Popacatapetl, I must admit the trainees didn't get that many marshalling-yards or heavy-water factories to recognise. Still, in wartime, improvisation itself becomes a virtue.

The other handicap I had to surmount was that as, in this remote corner, there was little else but scenery available in the way of off-duty pleasures, the Station had a thriving Camera Club. This meant that every moment of my spare time was taken up in developing and printing snaps for an entire squadron of keen amateur photographers.

It was this keenness which precipitated the awkward incident. For some time, the Flight Sergeant in charge of our Cookhouse had been paying court to a crofter's daughter named Ella McGivern. The only female in twenty-five square miles, she was an unprepossessing girl with a skin like a water-biscuit and legs like two vacuum-cleaner bags. Nevertheless, because of the sheer lack of competition, she functioned as our neighbourhood sex object.

For that reason, excitement ran high when it was

announced in DRO's that, on the following Friday evening, Ella had agreed to act as a live female model for the Camera Club. Fever pitch was reached when it became known, through less official channels, that the Flight Sergeant had persuaded her to pose in the nude.

In those days, of course, the word 'nude' was hardly the absolute term that it is today and Ella was insisting on retaining a pair of P. T. shorts below and a square of transparent net-curtaining up top. But when you've been the best part of eight months in a remote corner of Northern Scotland, even that is a fairly heady prospect.

Accordingly, come Friday, not only was the entire Camera Club to be seen clicking away at her but also a neighbouring platoon of Pioneer Corps, the complete intake of Intelligence Officers, all the sentries and two German parachutists.

For me, however, it meant only a virtually insuperable workload. For in addition to the task of developing single-handed all the figure studies of Ella that were snapped that evening, I also had to make ready an adequate supply of ten-by-eights for the official Aerial Photograph Inter-pretation Test which the C.O. had laid on for the Intelligence Officers the following morning.

The aerial photograph which I'd selected as the subject of the Test was of an area that, again, could hardly be described as a raging battleground. As time was short and the copies of the *National Geographic Magazine* were dwindling, I'd chosen a picture of a place called Karakorum, which is a mountain range in Tibet. As was my practice, I squared it off, selected an appropriate square and placed it under the enlarger.

At least, I think that's what I enlarged. To this day I can't be really sure. Bearing in mind that I also had in my Lab at the time three hundred or so Art Poses of Miss McGivern, the possibilities of error were considerable.

Mind you, the thought that I might have erred did not strike me until the following morning when the Test was already under way. I wandered in and watched the

Intelligence Officers scanning their ten-by-eights of what they'd been told was 'mountain terrain'. Only then did it occur to me that what they were all studying through their magnifying glasses might, conceivably, through sheer pressure of work and lack of sleep, be a monstrous enlargement of some section of Ella McGivern.

"Excuse me, sir." I tugged at the C.O.'s sleeve. "There is a possibility I may have made a boob."

The C.O. was a man who could have given irritability lessons to Captain Bligh. "Belt up, Corporal," he said. Then, to one of the Intelligence Officers - "Come on then, Pilot Officer Lacey. Make anything of it?"

Pilot Officer Lacey nodded confidently. "It's at least five thousand feet high," he said. "And there's cart tracks leading up the lower slopes."

"There's also traces of volcanic activity," volunteered a fellow Intelligence Officer. "And is that a small hut at the top?"

I could not, in all conscience, allow this to go on. I leant towards the C.O.'s ear and quietly confessed the possibility that I had submitted an error. Equally quietly he reduced me to AC2 and confined me to camp until 1957.

Then he turned to the officers. "I'm afraid the Test must be aborted, gentlemen," he said. "A certain measure of uncertainty has arisen regarding its subject matter."

With some distaste, he picked up a ten-by-eight. Surveying it, he said:

"This creation is Tibet, or part of Ella."

There's many a slip 'twixt the cup and the lip

Proverb

Frank

Paris was baking hot that May in 1863. The sun shone down, the temperature went up, tempers frayed, farmers prayed, the level of the Seine dropped, a revival of Gluck's opera *Iphigenia in Aulis* flopped, Sarah Bernhardt made her debut, people walking past drains went 'Pheew!', and the pavements were hot enough to *flamber* a crêpe-suzette on.

Idlers of the town strolling past Maxim's restaurant, picking their way carefully over the kneeling chefs and the suzettes, could only envy the rich courtesans who clip-clopped past in their open carriages, the moving air cooling their brows and disturbing such traces of lovely hair as escaped from beneath their characteristic, egg-shaped hats (*oeufs en cocottes*).

At a table in the Café de Bade, Émile Zola tried to stop the sweat dropping off his chin onto his manuscript as he put the finishing touches to his searing exposé of slavery in the banana plantations, *Nana*.

In a cheap bistro, a gaunt unhappy-looking English painter of draperies, by the name of Jack Hughes, put a paper doily on his head, balanced a silver sugar-sifter on top, puffed out his cheeks and said "Look everybody - Queen Victoria!" Few of his laughing fellow-artists guessed that his ambition was to become a leading Impressionist.

Perhaps the coolest spot in all Paris was beneath the great trees of the Bois de Boulogne. And it was there, in the very heart of the Bois, that the painter Édouard Manet was making his final attempt to win recognition. As he told his friends, "If the public does not like this last picture of mine I shall do myself, as the English say, in."

It was a beautiful setting for a painting. Manet had erected his easel in the shadow of a huge pile of granite boulders known to Parisians as Lover's Leap. There was grass, and trees, and in the background a pond full of carp which blew bubbles and swam about and did whatever mysterious things carp do to while away the time.

The picture was to be called *'Déjeuner sur l'herbe'* (Lunch is on Herbie), and was to depict Herbie giving a picnic lunch to a friend and a couple of girls. All of them nude. The nudity was partly to give the picture a neo-classical appeal but mostly because Manet was hopeless at painting dresses and pairs of trousers.

And so Manet painted furiously, while his mistress, Suzanne, and three friends sat with nothing on and tried to keep still.

"Herbie!" cried Manet, suddenly. "You're the host. You're supposed to be lolling at ease, chatting Suzanne. Why have you turned on to your left side?"

"Boil on me bum".

Manet muttered a Gallic imprecation.

More painting. Then:

"Ow!" from Suzanne. "Ow! Cor! Ow!"

"Now what?" from Manet.

"Ants! In the pants. Or where the pants would be if I was wearing any. Which thanks to you I'm not." She jumped up and danced about.

Manet gritted his teeth in exasperation. "I don't know why I keep you on as a model" he muttered.

"I do," she muttered back, "Judging from last night."

"What was that?"

"Nothing. Nothing."

More painting. Then Manet flung his brush down in exasperation.

"You, girl, whatever your name is!" he bellowed. "You're supposed to be reclining on one elbow on the grass. What are you doing back there in the pond?"

"Paddling!" she bellowed back. "Got a bunion. It's hard on a girl's feet in my profession."

Somehow, just one day before the picture had to be entered for the Salon, it was finished. Manet sent for his friend, Émile Zola, and waited, trembling, for his verdict.

"Sorry, Éd," said Zola, shaking his head sadly. "You have here a stinkeroo. A floperoo *formidable* (formidable). It's the nudes, old lad. Everybody's painted them this year. Nudes bathing, nudes up trees, nudes chasing each other round urns. Another nude painting doesn't stand a snowflake in hell's chance. Disappointing, I know, but I'm sure you want me, your old friend Zola, to be realistic."

Manet went white, including his ginger beard. "But there is no time to paint another!" he whispered. "And I can't paint clothes on to the figures - I can't DO clothes! This is *rideaux* (curtains) for me. Be so kind as to hand me that poison-bottle marked 'Poison' . . ."

"Wait!" cried Zola. "There must be a way . . ." He strode up and down for a while. Then he lifted a clenched fist to the ceiling and cried in a great voice, "*J'accuse! J'accuse!*" (Jack Hughes! Jack Hughes!)

"It is a name I have heard . . ."

"He is a gaunt, unhappy English painter who gives impersonations of Queen Victoria. But he is, my friend, a Drapery Man! You know, do you not, how those execrable English society portrait painters work? They paint in only the hands and the face and then engage a Drapery Man to paint in the clothes. Some hack like - Jack Hughes!"

The colour began to suffuse back into Manet's beard. "Suzanne!" He commanded. "Put some clothes on and fetch Jack Hughes!"

It was arranged within the hour. For the sum of ten francs, cash in advance, Hughes agreed to clothe the four figures in the painting.

"A nice pink dress for the girl paddling in the pond, if I might make a suggestion, sir," he said. "And a modish green muslin for the foremost bird. For the two gents I would suggest dark jackets and light trousers. With a smoking hat complete with tassel for the lad in the foreground." And he left.

Alas, how often in the history of Hope has the goblet been dashed from the lips before a drop of liquor had graced tonsil?

Hughes bought a bottle of absinthe with the ten francs and in three hours was as stewed as an eel. He managed to paint clothes on to the two men, but the paddling girl was left in what looked like a white underslip, and Suzanne was, as she usually was, stark naked. His landlady delivered the picture to the Salon.

Manet slipped into the Exhibition Hall the following night, but he only got as far as the door. The howls of rage and anger from the critics jostling round his picture were enough. He went very white. Whiter than white. And slipped away into the Paris night.

It's a pity he did not stay, really. An hour later a remarkable change had come over the gallery. Word had spread round the city that there was a beastly, degrading picture in the Salon and a hundred thousand excited art lovers were trying to batter their way in. And the artists of Paris had decided that Manet was an important pioneer in modern art, daring to combine classical nudes with fully-clothed figures in a contemporary setting.

Zola went round to Manet's studio to congratulate him, only to be met by a sobbing Suzanne. He put his arms round her to comfort her, and patted her.

"There, there, my dear," he said, "And, if you will permit an old friend, perhaps there?"

"Édouard has gone!" she sobbed, nodding. "He came

in, asked for his poison-bottle marked 'Poison' and rushed out again!''

Together they searched Paris. But nowhere did they find any trace of a pale-faced painter with a ginger beard carrying a poison-bottle.

"There is one tiny hope left," wheezed Zola as they climbed back up to Montmartre. "Put some clothes on, then we'll try the Bois de Boulogne. There's just a chance that he returned to the spot where he painted his picture."

And so they crept through the dark wood towards the little patch of grass between the granite bluff and the pond. Suzanne made Zola go on ahead, because of what he might find there.

What he found was a familiar figure, supine on the turf, motionless, clutching a small bottle. But not a poison-bottle marked 'Poison'. It was a quarter-bottle marked 'vin ordinaire'. And the figure was gently snoring.

Zola retraced his steps back to where Suzanne was anxiously waiting. "He grabbed the wrong bottle", he said.

"Then - '' she cried, "he has not done himself, as he has so frequently threatened to, in?"

"Indeed no," said Zola, pivoting her until she was facing the horizontal genius -

"There's Manet. Asleep. 'Twixt the carp and the Leap."

A stitch in time saves nine

Proverb

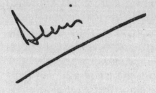

Looking back on my literary career, I think the most fulfilling period was when I was writing the Society Column for the *Barbers' and Hairdressers' Quarterly*. Although the work brought me into contact with most of the leading people in the trade, the one who has lingered longest in my memory is old Dino Goldoni.

A small, balding man, with a face like a melancholy knee-cap, he ran The Short Sharp Shave Shop, a two-chair lock-up off Camden Town High Street. His establishment owed its name to the fact that Dino, a three-time winner of the Masters Shaving Competition sponsored annually by my publication, had retired as undisputed champion of the art.

Now, however, he had received a challenge. A new man, a Greek called Andreas, whose saloon in Kensal Rise was the first to feature a basin into which you leaned *backwards* for a shampoo, had challenged Dino to a Shave Off.

For those of you unfamiliar with the rules of this contest, a Shave Off is a sudden-death competition in which two barbers vie with each other to see which can shave the most people over a given ten-minute period, any severed eyebrow or ear counting as two faults.

Old Dino, as the holder of three Golds, was fairly indulgent about the event at first. In the preceding week, he did put in a little practice on his backscrape, using as target his customary assistant, an Irishman called No Nose McGinty, but such was his confidence he spent little more than an hour a day at wrist-flexing and lather-rubbing. I must admit that I too regarded the occasion as no more than a work-out for Dino, even wondering a little at Andreas' temerity.

On the day of the Shave Off, however, my eyes were opened. As usual a guest manicurist had been brought in to act as Official Starter - in this case, a very popular girl called Florence, known throughout the trade as Cash Flo. My Editor and a man from the board of Silvikrin were along as judges. But just as Flo was about to drop the hot towel - the time-honoured signal for the start - Dino let out a startled yell. "Where's-a my brush? Who's-a swipe my brush?"

To the layman, the most important item of equipment in this kind of event would appear to be the razor. Not so. In competition shaving, the brush is all. Over years of use a barber will have moulded it to his individual hand, rendered it smooth and swift, learned just how much pressure to apply going round corners and across the cheekbone.

Now, at the crucial moment, Dino's brush had disappeared. When Andreas stepped forward smirking, I realised how dangerously we had underestimated him. Noting that he was clad, not in the grey overall of the old school, but in one of the new-fangled white nylon smocks, I reminded myself of the old adage: beware of Greeks wearing shifts.

"I claim a walkover," Andreas said with a white nylon smile. My Editor cocked an enquiring eye at Dino. He spread his hands miserably, acknowledging defeat.

"One moment, please," I said. "May I respectfully remind you of the BBC rules?" My Editor frowned but I held my ground. According to the official body which has

140

established the conventions for these events, the British Barbers' Committee, if a competitor loses an item of equipment, he is allowed fifteen minutes to replace it before being disqualified.

"Very well," said the Editor. "You have a quarter-of-an-hour." He started his stopwatch.

Dino shook his head hopelessly. "What's-a good?" he said (or possibly "What's a-good?"). "How'm I gonna find a good brush round these-a parts in fifteen minutes?"

"Listen," I said. "These-a parts are Camden Town. Right on the door-step of the London Zoo. Do you shave any of the keepers there?"

"My best customers," Dino said with a flash of the old pride. "They all-a come to Dino."

"Right," I replied. "Then we get on to the Head Keeper."

"What for do I need a Head Keeper?"

"Because it's a question of keeping your head. Seeing that there's no time to skin a badger, what's the next best animal for making a soft pliable shaving-brush?" When Dino shrugged in bewilderment, I pressed on urgently. "Ostrich feathers! The tail-feathers of an ostrich."

"He's-a not gonna pull all-a the feathers off his best ostrich just-a because Dino - "

"We're not asking him to," I interrupted. "Tell him to bring the ostrich itself along. Preferably a docile one."

Dino sighed and moved to the phone. It did take a certain amount of explaining on his part and roughly the same amount of expostulating on mine but, praise be, no more than twelve minutes had elapsed when the door opened and a tall sun-tanned man entered, leading an amiably-visaged ostrich.

I had a piece of twine ready waiting. It was the work of a moment to tie it round the ostrich's tail-feathers, pulling them tight so that they formed one uniform, manageable plume. As my Editor's fingers moved to his stop-watch knob to signal the end of our quarter-of-an-hour's grace, the plume was completed.

Down went Flo's hot-towel, and the contest was on. Into the shaving-mug went the plume, on to the customer's face went the lather - Dino was off and away.

Today, wherever men with cut-throats foregather, they still talk about Dino's performance that afternoon. Up till then, the world record for the ten-minute Shave Off had been seven customers. Dino did not simply break that record, he shattered it. The new figure he established still stands.

As I mentioned earlier, in terms of emotional experience it was one of the most fulfilling episodes of my life. Whenever the bad times come now, or the old fire flickers, I still summon up remembrance of the phrase I headlined my story with:

"Ostrich And Twine Shaves Nine."

A jug of wine, a loaf of bread - and thou

Omar Khayyám
'Rubaiyat'

Well, Jeremy, I understand from your aunty that you are going to be married to that nice girl in the gas showroom. No, I wouldn't agree that she is all that enormous. A little bulky, perhaps, particularly when she is demonstrating an oven, but no doubt once safely married she will moderate her present enthusiasm for eating things like chocolate fudge and cold roast potatoes.

How wise you are to get your ferrets used to new sleeping quarters; I think you should consider moving them right out of your bedroom now that they have got used to not sleeping in your bed.

Faintly on the same theme, I have a word of warning to you. It has been said that a bride's attitude towards her betrothed can be summed up in three words: Aisle. Altar. Hymn. You must prepare to resist alteration in those areas where a change is not an improvement.

It may come as a shock to you when you are married so perhaps now is the time to prepare yourself mentally to face a generally acknowledged fact; most women have an eccentric attitude towards personal hygiene.

For instance, women tend to underestimate, some of them by weeks, how long a pair of socks can be worn before they need to be changed.

Brides also fail to appreciate that when a man's hands become soiled, say through dismantling a carburettor or shifting a heap of coal, Dame Nature has provided absorbent matter for him to wipe his hands on in the shape of drying-up cloths, bathroom towels, and the edges of tablecloths. You will find that this natural practice will be frowned upon.

But much more important, and in some cases downright dangerous, is the feminine insistence that the male should wallow in a hot bath at least once a week.

The bath is not a British thing, Jeremy. Like a lot of other things, such as polo, cats, markets and carpets, it was imported from ancient Persia. However, the Persian version had an additional attraction; it was mixed bathing.

The bath next cropped up in ancient Greece. Mrs Archimedes used to fill her husband's bath right up to the brim. Archimedes found that the water slopped over the sides when he jumped in, and by weighing the amount of water spilt, and weighing himself, he discovered a formidable argument against baths, or at least full ones, in that a floating body displaces its own weight of water. He also discovered that the displaced water wet the bath-towel and made it so heavy that when he hung it on the towel-rail it pulled out the nails and the rail fell off the wall. So he invented the screw.

The idea of washing one's person seems to have been introduced into England during the reign of Henry II by a cleric of advanced views who used to give himself an all-over wash in a pail. He became known as Thomas O'Bucket.

The full obsession with immersing the body in the alien element came into fruition in Victorian times. They had a motto then, 'Cleanliness is Next to Godliness' - a sentiment about as logical as 'Lawn-mowing is Next to Madrigal-Singing'.

Consider the matter from a scientific point of view. Your skin is like a Fair Isle sweater (yours more than most people's, Jeremy, but I am sure the blotches are mostly due

144

to nerves). Think of yourself as entirely covered in a kind
of knitted garment which keeps your bones in place. Itto
nerves). Think of yourself as entirely covered in a kind of
knitted garment which keeps your bones in place. It has
neat edging round the lips to stop your mouth from
fraying, and has some loose embroidery on top which we
call hair. And like a Fair Isle sweater, it is a living,
breathing thing, full of natural oils. Now if you soak this
continually in hot water, and rub it all over with a cake of
chemical substance made from rancid grease boiled up
with caustic soda, then the natural protective oils will be
washed away and all sorts of things will happen, beginning
with colds and chills and ending with the skin shrinking,
moisture getting in and, eventually, rusty ribs.

My own plan for personal cleanliness is simplicity itself
and entirely in concord with nature.

Once a week - or so - stand naked in the bath and dab
yourself lightly all over with a bit of cotton wool moistened
in rainwater. Don't use tapwater, which has chemicals and
impurities in it to make it taste nice. Keep an old jug handy
and stick it under a drain pipe, or the down pipe of a
gutter, so that you have a supply of rainwater always to
hand.

Areas of mud, axle-grease, dried paint, and tar should
be given individual treatment with a loofah. Not a wet
loofah, which is flabby and useless, but a dry loofah.
Scrub away hard until the offending matter is dislodged,
pausing only if you find that you are about to draw blood.

For the final toning up, rub yourself down with a slice of
stale bread, using a circular motion and no butter. Bread
has the property of absorbing water and grease, and eras-
ing any pencil marks you might have overlooked.

Dash about a bit on the bathroom lino to dry off and the
job is done, using pure, natural means.

So, Jeremy, take a firm stand on the question of frequent hot baths, which are foreign, pagan, and dangerous.
All your bride needs for a clean and decent husband is four
things:

A jug of rain, a loofah, bread - and thou.

He who hesitates is lost

Proverb

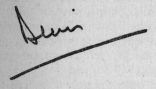

Those Kung Fu entertainments are an intriguing blend of bone-fracture and sententiousness. I was watching one the other night where the hero - a right prosy beggar, but the owner of a lethal left leg - observed to the baddie, "The man who loves unhappily will never finish first in the obstacle-race of Life." Then he kicked him in the groin and rode off into the commercial.

His remark, however, stayed with me. "Could that possibly account for it?" I mused. "Could that explain my own failure to break Life's tape ahead of the field?" For when I catalogue the various romantic attachments which have decorated my days - nights were generally out of the question, they had to wash their hair - the list does emerge as a pretty miserable series of encounters.

It's possibly because I started off on the wrong foot, if that's the correct anatomical referent in these matters. My adolescence, you see, was too early for what's become known as the sexual revolution. In fact, when I was seventeen, there appeared to be a sexual cease-fire. True, a roped-off section of the lending library called 'Modern' Novels offered the odd inflammatory chapter-ending, but you had to be twenty-five before you could borrow one and even then it was two old-pence per day. And when I did once manage to nail a book called *Learn to Love,* it turned out to be the sixth volume of a set of encyclo-paedias, the next volume being *Luana to Membrane.*

So, with no Dr Reuben or Martin Cole around to direct our urges, what the panting young oicks of my era adopted as behaviour-models were the sentimental Hollywood films of that period. I grew to manhood fully believing that all girls shut their eyes when kissed on the lips, most of them standing on tiptoe with one leg bent upwards. And, at my most impressionable period, a scene in one of those films - a Charles Boyer/Jean Arthur romance - left an absolutely indelible imprint.

I can see that scene now. They were dining in a fashion-able restaurant and, coffee having arrived, Boyer beckoned. A strolling violinist entered the scene and, leaning over Jean Arthur, he softly played their particular our-tune into her left ear. And as she listened, her hand involuntarily stole across the table and her little finger linked into his. (Into Charles Boyer's I mean. Had it been the violinist's, it would, of course, have cocked-up the melody-line utterly.)

Well, I can't tell you to what heights of dewy-eyed soppiness that moment sent me. To the sort of male I was then - and, if truth be told, have been ever since as well - all of romance was in that scene. "If only," I thought, "if only I could arrange an identical set-up for myself, Life need strew no other rose in my path."

For more than one reason it wasn't easy. Snag A was that no restaurant in my postal district featured a strolling musician; Snag B, there was no girl I fancied anywhere near strongly enough to buy a whole meal for. However, within a month both A and B were taken care of.

First, right next door, a new family moved in containing an eminently molestable daughter called Lily. For the statistically-minded, her measurements were 36, 24, 36, 27; the last figure being her I.Q. But so besotted was I by the other three numerals I cared not. The other happy circum stance was that the haberdashers in the High Street closed

147

down and reopened - after some initial difficulties with the spelling of the neon sign - as 'The Hendon Brasserie'. More important, it was owned and personally managed by an ex-member of Bram Martin's Orchestra. Anticipating the imminent demise of the Big Bands, he had decided to invest his savings in something less transitory.

So I had it all going for me - the place, the girl, the strolling violinist. Getting Lily to agree to 'date' me, as the operation was then called, proved easier than I anticipated and when she met me at the Brasserie she looked a knock-out. Admittedly she appeared to be about two foot taller than when I'd last seen her but that was because of the hairdo that girls of that day adopted for formal occasions - a sort of black-gloss beehive. She proved to have a healthy appreciation of food so there was little conversation through the three-course table d'hôte, Lily being occupied in stuffing herself like an out-of-work taxidermist. But when coffee was finally served, she pushed away from the table and looked at me for the first time. Taking it to be a good augury that she was still breathing quite heavily, I moved in closer. "What's your favourite tune?" I asked, giving her the Franchot Tone turned-down-on-one-side smile.

As I mentioned earlier, she was a bit hard of thinking so there was quite a pause before the answer. "I beg yours?" she said.

"Your favourite tune."

"Oh, I'm not all that musical really." She pondered. "What's the one that goes - " and she hummed a few bars.

"That's the National Anthem," I said. "Tell you what, I'll pick one." And beckoning the manager-violinist over, I said "Listen, my good fellow. Can you play 'Time After Time I Tell Myself That I'm'?"

He nodded and winked. Then, leaning forward to Lily's ear, he began - on that low, sexy string they hardly ever seem to use any more. I locked my eyes into Lily's and awaited developments. She was still blowing a bit but, sure enough, after no more than a half-chorus, her hand came creeping across the table.

As I found out afterwards, it was only groping for a toothpick, but no matter. I seized her little finger, curled my own little finger into it, gripped tight, and closed my eyes in bliss. Pure and unalloyed bliss.

In fact, so utter was the bliss that when the music ceased playing, I didn't even notice it at first. It was only when I heard a strange kind of *sawing* noise. . . .

He'd somehow got his violin-bow stuck right through her beehive! Remember how peculiarly unyielding the lacquer was that girls used in those days? If you ever ran your fingers through their hair you stood a fair chance of breaking your nails. Well, this clown, this poop, he'd managed to push his bow right into the interior. And now the resin had somehow *bonded* itself to . . . oh, it was just so dispiriting, so awful, I can't even bear recalling any more of it.

Anyway, when that's the kind of foot a fellow gets started off on in the romance line, you do see how miserably his later liaisons are going to turn out. And so it proved. That's why that line of Kung Fusion set me brooding so much. "The man who loves unhappily will never finish first in the obstacle-race of Life."

Or if you prefer the Western version:

"He who has sad dates is last."

None was for a party; all were for the state

Lord Macaulay
Lays of Ancient Rome: 'Horatius'

Frank

The only bit of Spanish I remember after wrestling with it for a term at school is an ancient proverb which went: 'Whoever Spitteth at Heaven Shall Have it Fall Back in his Eye.' A good thought; cautionary, ballistically sound. And it seems to me that we should have a similar proverb in English to warn the impulsive of the dangers of doing the opposite; not spitting at Heaven but trying to get a bit nearer to it. I propose the following: 'Whoever Foolishly Attempteth to Bring About a Social Reform Very Likely will Find that it Falleth Upon Cloth Ears and Lo the Ground Will be Stony and Before He Knoweth Where He is He Will be Back Where He Started having Achieved Sweet Fanny Adams and Made to Feel an Utter Nana.'

That's only the first draft, of course. It will need honing before it goes into *The Oxford Dict. of Eng. Proverbs.*

The need for such a proverb was brought home to me recently when I attempted to set on its way a small but, it seemed to me, vital social reform.

The Classless Society is the dearest wish of all of us but spreading the word that beans-on-toast are chic and Rolls-Royces are heavy on brake-linings is only nibbling at the problem. There is one real bastion of class-consciousness which must be removed.

Until recently the main Class giveaways were speech and dress. If somebody spoke a little too loudly, with a pre-war BBC announcer's accent, keeping the vowels well open, then he or she was an Upper. If all this was attempted and it just failed, then he or she was a Middle. Mumbling mangled vowels, and local colour in the accent indicated Lower. But nowadays, thanks to telly, pop-music, and the media generally, our youth and our trendier middle-aged now talk what might be termed Standard Received Disc-Jockey. If you meet a lad in Windsor High Street it is now no longer possible to tell from his speech whether he is Eton or Slough Comprehensive.

Clothes have also ceased to be reliable indicators of Class. If you spot a little riot of colour ambling along the King's Road it could well be the rhythm guitarist of The Who. It could also be The Right Hon. Leo Abse M.P. on his way to the opening of Parliament.

But there is still one infallible way of separating the sheep from the lambs, the ewes from the non-ewes, and that is what we call the place where we all, from time to time, are compelled to go. Roughly speaking, Uppers goto the Lavatory, Middles to the Loo and Lowers go to the Toilet.

This is oversimplifying the picture to an enormous extent; in fact, the situation is in a state of flux. Loo is holding its own fairly well but there is a strong, perhaps 14%, swing to Toilet and most of these gains are at the expense of Lavatory.

These terms are totally non-interchangeable in society. Uppers and Middles recoil from the vulgarity of the word 'Toilet'. Uppers and Lowers both regard 'Loo' as being a hopelessly twee euphemism. And Lowers and Middles join in finding the aristocratic use of the word 'Lavatory' utterly disgusting.

Now it wouldn't be too bad if we had just those three words - the U.S.A. manages happily with two, the John and the Can - but unfortunately we have a great many more words for the Unmentionable Thing. Consequently when strangers meet in an English house, and nature calls, our society breaks into a *mille-feuille* of scoial strata, the guest trying frantically to sort out in his mind which euphemism his host is most likely to embrace and the host similarly trying to fit euphemism to guest.

Many older hosts and hostesses, who grew up in a protected, non-permissive society, can't bear to apply any word at all to It. They say, "Would you like to . . . (faint upward wave of right hand) . . .?" Or simply, "Are you . . . all right?"

School-children are brought up to avoid a confrontation by being taught to use such evasions as "Please, Miss, may I be excused?" "Please, Sir, may I leave the room?" The confusion which this produces in the delicate, growing mind is illustrated by the small boy who suddenly put his hand up and said "Please, Miss, Johnny's left the room on the floor".

Keen euphemismaticians often study a stranger's house for clues before taking the plunge. Framed prints of vintage cars on the walls, pewter tankards, and "Match of the Day" on the telly indicate an approach along the lines of:

"Where's the geography, old son?" Or:

"Excuse me, but I must go and see whether my horse has kicked off its blanket".

(*Note:* These phrases are rarely necessary as this host invariably greets his guests with a cheerful, "By the way, the bog's on the landing".)

Colour Supplements lying about, Hi-Fi, and Spanish Claret indicate a slightly more roguish approach from the host:

"Ah - if anyone needs the House of Lords it's at the end past the au-pair's room." Or:

"Comforts anyone?"

And in between these phrases there are a hundred others, each one clung to by a section of the population as being the one socially acceptable phrase which will protect them from hideous embarrassment.

Obviously something must be done to straighten this situation out, and the answer to the problem is to find a word for the Thing which is acceptable to all ranks. But which word? 'Lavatory' is useless; it is the word plumbers use for washbasin. 'Toilet' is a horrid euphemism, imported from the U.S.A., which really means a lady's dressing-table. 'Loo' doesn't mean anything at all, being a hangover from eighteenth-century Edinburgh when folks were wont to empty their chamber pots out of the top stories of tenement buildings with a cheerful warning cry of, "Guardy-loo!"

The problem was solved for me one evening when a small, round, innocent face looked up into mine and said, simply, "I want potty". It wasn't a child who spoke, in fact, it was a shortish Rural Dean who had come round about a subscription and had stayed to bash the sherry. But the simple, child's word 'Potty' was the word I had been searching for. An old, honourable, easily remembered word, and the only word of the whole bunch which described the Thing itself.

My mind went immediately into overdrive (unhappily, I recall, forgetting the Rural Dean and his pressing problem) and it seemed to me that I should form a society to promote the use of the word 'Pot'. Perhaps calling the society Pioneers of Truth (thus making clever use of the initial letters), with myself as (paid) President. Perhaps I would write the society a brief, expensive manifesto. . . .

I saw the Rural Dean out of the front door and into the bushes and immediately sat down and wrote out a questionnaire, to send to a hundred people to test whether I had judged the people's mood correctly. I asked them to state clearly whether they would be in favour of everybody settling to call the Thing something like 'Potty' rather than messing about pretending that they were nipping outside to check whether the trusty steed had kicked off its saddle.

It was when the results of my referendum were all in that I realised a sad truth. A truth encapsulated in the proverb

153

'Whoever Folishly Attempteth to Bring About a Social Reform Very Likely Will Find that it Falleth Upon Cloth Ears . . . (etc.)' The figures are conclusive:

None was for a Potty; all were for The Steed.

The rank is but the guinea's stamp

Robert Burns
'For a' that and a' that'

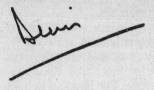

Yes, I've had some odd experiences in Gents' Loos - I still chuckle at what happened when I used the one in the Leaning Tower of Pisa - but the oddest, I think, occurred behind the door marked 'Maharajahs' at a certain well-known Indian restaurant in Mayfair.

Immediately upon entering its marble vastness, my attention was caught by the behaviour of a tall, red-headed gentleman. Standing in front of a mirror, he was inspecting himself keenly, all the while nodding his head rapidly up and down, then shaking it equally forcefully to and fro. After watching his vigorous nodding-and-shaking for some several minutes, I could no longer restrain my curiosity. "Excuse me, sir," I said. "Are you in the throes of some deep internal conflict?"

"I fear my dilemma is of a more external nature," he replied. "I am endeavouring to ascertain just how far - look, sir, perhaps you can enlighten me." Performing some further agitations of his head, he asked, "When I go like this, do you chance to notice any marked alteration of my visage?"

I gazed at him intently. Finally, "Yes." I replied. "Your forehead appears to - diminish."

He sighed heavily. "As I feared," he said. Then

155

seating himself upon the chinchilla top of the used paper towel basket, he told me his story.

At a very early age he had had the misfortune to lose his hair. Not all of it, but enough to impart to his scalp in adult life a kind of see-through look. It had rendered him acutely, and perhaps unduly, sensitive about his appearance; to such an extent that he had, as far as was possible, shunned all contact with the opposite sex.

As he was a gynaecologist by trade, such a withdrawal had proved as damaging professionally as it was socially. However, quite recently a patient's husband had drawn his attention to a startling advance in masculine embellishment: the false hairpiece, or toupée. On impulse he had purchased one - a red one - and after trying it on, he adjudged his appearance so enhanced that he took courage in both hands and joined a mixed pot-holing group.

There, while descending a narrow chimney, he had found himself sitting on the nose of an extremely pleasing younger lady. Their acquaintanceship had ripened and now, after some months of courtship, he had invited her here to this caravanserai of curry with the express purpose of asking her to become his wife.

"And does she know about your false roof?" I broke in at this point. "Have you told her that you are, as it were, carrying on business under an assumed mane?"

He shook his head mournfully - causing another slight subsidence of the thatch. "I have not yet summoned up courage," he said. "That is why what happened during the dessert course was so dismaying. I had chosen the Gooseberry Compôte and when she asked me whether she could have my glacé cherry, I nodded my head. As I did so, suddenly I felt this unaccustomed current of air upon my cranium."

"It fell off?" Involuntarily my voice rose, for there can be few mental images more chilling than that of an upside-down red toupée in a plate of stewed gooseberries.

"Fortunately no. But it did make a significant skid forward. Happily she didn't notice, being fully occupied

156

with her Rum Baba. So, making a trumped-up excuse, I hastened here. And now - well, now every movement seems to loosen it further. See?'' He made a nodding movement again, causing another manifestation of what astronomers call, I believe, the Red Shift. "What's happened, you see, is something for which I have only myself to blame. You must understand that these things are held firm to the head by means of a strip of sticking-plaster which one is supposed to renew daily. Tonight though, such was my excitement, I neglected to effect the renewal. In consequence, unless I can now find some other means of adhesion, it's - farewell, Rozella!''

"Is that what you call it?" I asked.

That's the young lady's name. Sir, can you perhaps suggest something by which I may anchor it?''

"Well, if all you need is a sticking-plaster, surely that First Aid Cabinet on the wall, the one with the minarets? Something in there - ?''

"I have already searched it. It has everything but sticking-plaster. Bandages, lint, iodine - even splints.''

"Bandages!'' I said. "What about going back with your head covered in bandages? Say that on your way here, some indigent immigrant mugged you for your lighter fuel.''

"One can hardly propose in a turban. Especially not in an Indian restaurant. Have you, perhaps, something about your person?''

I explored my pockets. "Nothing I'm afraid. Tell you what, though. In my brief-case I've got some drawing-pins. Couldn't we try to . . . no, perhaps not. What's really needed is some kind of adhesive substance, isn't it. Look, I say, here's a thought. Suppose you go back to the table and tell the waiter you've gone off the idea of stewed goose-berries, you really fancy a baked apple. Then when he brings it, you fetch it in here. Baked apple, you see, always has that toffee-bit on top. Sometimes that's of quite start-ling stickiness.''

"But won't Rozella question my reason for taking a baked apple into the Gentlemen's Toilet?''

"Let her. In any relationship there have to be certain areas of privacy. Mind you - "

"What?"

"I don't think Indian restaurants serve baked apple."

His face, which had brightened, fell again. Don't despair," I said. "Not yet." I hardened my eyes and gazed upwards, a habit I have when concentrating. "No use staring at the ceiling, boy," my old Maths Master used to say. "You won't find the answer up there." It never crossed his mind that I'd sneaked in the night before and scribbled out the Trig. tables all round the light fitting.

The ceiling! Wait a minute, when was it? Last Christmas? Yes! The pennies! Ten pounds in pennies!

"Just wait here," I said to my toupéed friend and hurried out. Within three minutes I was back. "Ever been in a pub that's collecting for a favourite charity?" I panted. "They stick the pennies you contribute up on the ceiling. Know how? With *this*!" And I held up the bottle of stout I'd just purchased from the little off-licence down the street. "So if we just pour out a little, then moderately dampen the inside of your wig with it. . . ."

Two months later a small box came through my letter-box. Inside was a rather stingy piece of wedding cake.

Since that evening, I never see an advert for those hirsute artifices without recalling my friend's last-minute repair job and I wonder whether other users of hairpieces ever find themselves relying upon a similar emergency fixative. I hope not. For how precariously perched must such crowning glories be, when - in Burns' phrase -

"Their anchor's but the Guinness damp".

O, for the wings, for the wings of a dove

Mendelssohn
'Hear My Prayer'

Frank

There has been a lot of loose talk going on in places where
thinking men congregate, like the fruit-machine salon at
the Athenaeum Club and the House of Commons Sauna
and Massage Parlor, as to why Britain has declined to the
status of a second-class power.

Ignoring for a moment the fact that many of us see
nothing disastrous in this - dropping from being Top Dog,
with all the duties and responsibilities which go with it, to
being Number Two can be a merciful release, as many a
husband knows - the reason for this supposed decline in
Britain's might seems to be in doubt. Various reasons have
been advanced.

On the global level my researches have revealed the
following: America thinks we are bankrupt. Scotland
thinks we have too much money. Japan thinks we are too
tall. Mr Enoch Powell thinks we are too tinted. Germany
thinks our working-class doesn't work. Russia thinks our
working-class is crushed by the rich. Switzerland thinks
that according to her standards we haven't got any rich.
The Confederation of British Industries thinks we are
trapped between the Devil and the TUC.

On the more local level I have had meaningful dialogue
with a retail-outlet contact; a piece of trendy jargon

meaning I spent an hour trotting behind Mercer the milkman as, whiff ablaze, he strode round the village bestowing pintas on doorsteps. According to Mercer, who has a fine ear for this sort of thing, local opinion holds that the sad state of the nation is attributable to one or more of the following reasons: they are putting fluoride in the water at Staines reservoir; the new motorway workings have fractured the pipes leading to Lyne Lane sewage farm and the stuff is leaking into the soil; there was a shortage of bees last summer; it's the rubbish on the telly.

All these might be contributory factors but the whole lot together would only add up to a temporary *cafard*, not a national decline. No, the real reason is more fundamental. In my opinion the decline of the British nation as a great power is directly connected with the decline in our consumption of boiled pudding.

It is an undeniable fact that our nation began to lose its pre-eminence at the same time as the good, old-fashioned steamed suet pudding fell into desuetude.

I am prepared to support my theory with facts. In medieval times the Englishman, be he noble or lewd, stood about five feet in height and, because vegetables were not invented until the eighteenth century, went to an early grave riddled with scurvy. So where did he get the energy to win at Agincourt? From boiled puddings. For centuries the ability of the English to consume boiled puddings was a matter of wonder to continentals. What hope had French and Spanish troops, fed on hot water with stringy bits of meat floating about in it, against our English bowman, belts bursting with good pudding; suet to keep out the cold and damp, flour for bulk, and meat for energy?

Almost everything was shoved into the puddings to begin with; veal, pork, mutton, various interior organs of the deer, but latterly, from the eighteenth century, puddings came to be eaten more and more as puddings and were stuffed with plums or coated with jam.

At the height of the British Empire our public schools supplied a stream of splendid chaps to the administrators in those far-flung countries coloured red on the map. Straight from boarding-school they went, honking with adenoids, and after five years of digesting roly-poly puddings and figgy duffs, constipated to the eyebrows and thus impervious to dysentry.

All gone now, of course; both the red bits on the map and puddings. Since the last war puddings have been called 'sweets' and usually consist of either a mess of artificially tinted and flavoured froth, or a baleful mixture of semi-edible substances called something like Baked Caramel and Mallow Ring.

An honest worker queues up for his pud in the canteen and orders Manchester Tart. What is dumped on his plate is a wedge-shaped piece of thickish, warm cardboard lightly smeared with raspberry flavoured red lead. Hardly the sort of fodder to send him whistling back to Blast Furnace No. 2 replete and raring to go.

And then there's the Prime Minister. Flying to Moscow for a vital talk with the Soviet Premier. On the way they serve lunch. And what do they find him for pud on the plane? Half a tinned apricot resting on a bed of soggy rice. How can he stand up for us against the might of Russia with only that under his belt?

Ah, where are the puds of yesteryear? Spotted Dick; fine, crusty suet pudding studded with a galaxy of plum currants. Boiled Baby; heavy, densely-textured pudding boiled in a cloth. A characteristic soft coating, known to aficionados as 'the slime' was scraped gently off the outside before the pudding was anointed with very hot golden syrup. Figgy Duff: the Prince of Suet Puddings, very popular in the Royal Navy, both as food and for pressing into service as keel ballast, emergency anchor, or ammunition for the cannons. An inch-and-a-half slice of a good Figgy Duff weighed about three and a quarter pounds.

But I suppose what we old Figgy Duff and Boiled Baby fanciers miss most of all is that unique physical sensation which set in when one had eaten that delicious little bit too

161

much pudding. It was like a pain, except that it wasn't a pain. The tum, which before the pudding had been soft and flexible, became tight as a drum and firm enough to crack a flea on. And an odd, charming ache, halfway between a spasm of wind and an old-fashioned twinge, made its presence felt. The medical name for it was the 'winge'. And it was the most satisfying feeling in the world.

Coming home from a restaurant or a dinner-party nowadays my wife may say something like:

"Wasn't that Apple-peel and Ginger Mousse good? I feel absolutely full." Or, "Did you like the Marinated Passion-Fruit and Marshmallow Whip? I don't think I'll need another meal for a week!"

I agree with her, of course. But in my heart of hearts I know that at that moment I am missing something; something beautiful which has gone forever. And I think to myself:

"O, for the winge, for the winge of a duff!"

In the great right of an excessive wrong

Robert Browning
'The Ring and the Book'

There is little point in going into the reasons why Frank
and I found ourselves running a Matrimonial Agency. It
was, I suppose, a panic attempt to restore our finances
after the failure of our first play, a sensitive social allegory
about a black mermaid. But when, after eight months'
trading, our Agency still only had two clients on its books,
I was all for packing it in and turning the place into a
massage parlour. ("Everyone likes to feel kneaded" was
the argument I used.)

But Frank is made of more determined stuff. "All we
have to do is show results." he said. "If we could just fix
up the two we've got with *each other*. . . !" And he drew
from his roll-top desk the well-thumbed dossiers of our
only two supporters.

We gazed at their photographs with some gloom. The
male client was named Jack Longland - no relation, just
one of those happy coincidences. He was a slightly-built
man, no more than five-foot-one in height. The lady was
one Emma Williamson, six-foot-four and a good sixteen
stone.

Surveying them side by side, even Frank's resolve
wavered. "It's like trying to mate a pram and a furniture
van," he said. I felt my own spirits droop like a wax

163

banana in a heat wave. "I doubt whether Henry Kissinger could bring these two together."

"We have to try," said Frank firmly and picked up the telephone. In such circumstances, the first step is for each partner to be summoned to the Agency and there shown a photograph of the other. If, in both cases, the prospect pleases, then we arrange what is known in the trade as a 'meet'.

Emma presented us with no difficulties. In her early forties - her *late* early forties - she was far enough down the home-stretch to settle for practically anything with the right hormones. "Twelve years now I've been on the Pill," she confided. "And if I don't get talking to somebody soon. . . ."

It was Jack who proved to be the recalcitrant partner. Possessing, like most small men, an acute sense of personal dignity, he was immediately sensitive to the disparity in their respective square footages. "Great ugly fat lump," he said when I displayed Emma's picture. "Put her in a white dress, you could show films on her."

Fortunately Frank is the type who could sell bagels to the Arab League. "Looks aren't everything, Jack," he argued. "And, anyway, beauty fades. But a big plain girl, Jack - she stays big and plain forever." It took a deal of persuasion but Jack was finally talked into accepting Emma's invitation to a whirl round the Planetarium the following Saturday afternoon.

In this, as in their subsequent get-togethers, it was Emma who made the running. She it also was who phoned in progress reports after each meeting. The first few were bleak indeed. "We spent an evening at Battersea Fun Fair," was one of her early bulletins. "In the Tunnel Of Love, he insisted on separate carriages."

On the few occasions that Jack dropped in to pay his subs, we found ourselves committed to long sessions of reassurance and rebuttal. "But she's so enormous," he'd protest. "In that lurex dress, it's like being out with a giant Brillo pad."

"Don't keep dwelling on Emma's bad points," Frank would plead. "Think *benefits*! Warmth in the winter and shade in the summer!"

Finally, against all odds, it began to happen. The first hint was an excited message from Emma. "Last night," she exclaimed, "last night he hung up on me so gently, it was almost a caress."

When Jack came into the office the next morning, the change in his demeanour was unmistakable. "Well," he said, "I never thought I would but I have."

"Emma?" I asked eagerly.

He nodded and smile slightly. "I've fallen for that mountain of womanhood."

"Oh well done, Jack," Frank said warmly. "Accept our sincere condolences for your future happiness."

"Dunno about getting that far," Jack said. A muscle in his cheek twitched. "Did you know she's also a bit mutt-and-jeff?"

Well, we were aware that Emma had a slight hearing problem but it was not something we'd emphasised, any more than a car dealer will go out of his way to show the wear on the rear tyres. "Could well put a spoke in the whole shooting-match, that could," Jack went on unhappily. "I mean, how do I set about proposing to her? If I go down on the knee and ask her, it could well happen that due to the inordinate distance between my mouth and her ears she won't hear a blind word. And I'm not going to kneel there shouting it. I don't hold with small-built men shouting."

Behind his glasses his eyes blinked miserably, giving him the appearance of an evicted owl. Frank and I exchanged glances. We had come to respect the little man's sensitivity towards his lack of tall, so we saw the need to tread carefully.

Then Frank narrowed his eyes and tapped the side of his nose at me. It was a gesture which meant, I recalled from our Paul Newman/Robert Redford games, he'd had an idea.

"Jack," he said. "Let me show you what we use to clean that light-fitting up on the ceiling." He crossed the room and opened the broom cupboard. Withdrawing from it a folding ladder, he said. "We use this. Jack, go thou and do likewise."

"Do what?"

"Take the ladder away, Jack. Take it round to Emma's flat, stand it at her side and climb to its topmost rung. Then make your proposal from there."

Jack's blinking slowed momentarily then became even more agitated. "But a gentleman can't go clambering about ladders in a lady's drawing room. What if she asks *why* I'm climbing up it?"

"Tell her - because it's there."

Frank still avers that it could have worked and it should have worked. All I know is it didn't work. Immediately we received Emma's distraught phone-call, we sped round to her basement flat. There, in the fireplace, lay Jack's limp and broken form.

I deduced instantly what had happened. After taking the ladder and measuring it against Emma's length, my suspicions were confirmed. The ladder was too long.

Jack, in his joyous haste, had rushed up it so fast he'd gone one rung too many, shot clean over her head, and landed in the fireplace. Now he lay where he had fallen:

In the grate, right off an excessive rung.

Come into the garden, Maud

Alfred, Lord Tennyson
'Maud'

Frank

I must have been about nine at the time of the tragedy; a
wiry, quiet lad, much given to solitary walks and Uncle
William's Banana-Flavour Toffee.

They were long, hot summers at Broadstairs in those
days. A military band played in the bandstand on the
promenade, Uncle Mac performed his Minstrel Show on
the beach twice daily, and the 'Perseverance', smelling
excitingly of diesel oil fumes, took trippers for a sick round
the bay.

All day was spent on the beach. I wore a bathing
costume, bathing hat, and plimsolls from dawn to dusk,
wet or fine. The costume was my pride; the acme of chic
men's beachwear around the year 1929; the top half was
like a vest, with horizontal hoops of maroon, and - a
design featurette - large holes below the normal armholes.
Then working southwards, came an imitation belt with a
rusty buckle, and a navy-blue lower half complete with a
modesty skirt.

The bathing hat, which was worn at all times, was made
of some intractable black rubber, possibly from old tractor
inner-tubes, about a quarter of an inch thick. It had rubber
ear-pieces welded on, into which the ears were supposed to
repose snugly. Because I had found the hat on the beach

my ears did not quite coincide and so not only was much agony endured but my ears are now about half an inch farther forward than is normal.

I found myself attracted more and more to the pier end of the beach, where the boats were moored. This now has a concrete slipway and a brass plate reading 'Edward Heath Slipped Here' but in those days there was just a lot of seaweed and a few moored dinghies gently banging into each other. What with the seaweed and the toffee papers and the Choc-Ice wrappers it was not so much messing about in boats as boating about in mess.

Very soon the Dinghy Set had accepted me as a sort of mascot and I spent all my time with them. Sometimes one of them would take me out for a sail and let me lower the centre-board and do a bit of bailing, and I would run all the way home, ten feet tall, freezing cold, with a soaking wet bottom.

They were all very much older than me. My particular hero was the group's acknowledged leader, Guy Beauchamp, a middle-aged man of about twenty-two. Most of the others shared a boat between them but Guy had his own, which he worked on all day, touching up varnish and tightening the stays. I spoke very little in those days. Not because I was timid but because I usually had a chunk of Uncle William's toffee in my mouth and as the toffee was broken off a block with a toffee-hammer and the pieces were usually large, pointed triangles which almost pierced the cheeks, any attempt at speech usually resulted in the listener being drenched with a fine spray of banana-flavour juice. But Guy spoke even less than I did. His conversation seemed to be entirely restricted to laconic, one-word instructioins; 'Anchor', he would say. And perhaps an hour later, 'Oar'. He had fair hair, a cleft in his chin, and he wore khaki shorts which came just below the knee and a roll-neck sweater apparently knitted from spaghetti. He pottered about in the water all day getting his feet wet and never caught cold. A tremendously impressive chap.

His girl friend was Carmen Rowbottom, the iron-monger's daughter, although Mr Rowbottom called it 'row-both-am' because he had married the gas manager's daughter and was a sidesman. I could never see much to Carmen at the time. She was quite elderly, pushing twenty, and wasn't very interesting to look at, having rather a lot of loose hair, like a carthorse's ankle, and huge bumps above her waist which got in the way when she rowed. But Guy was very keen on her, taking her for long, silent sails.

At the other end of the scale was Charlie Gordon who worked as a reporter on the *East Kent Messenger*. He was known as 'Toothy' because he hadn't got many, due to a cricket-ball. Toothy was small, bow-legged and ugly. He spent most of the time sitting on the edge of the pier, not helping, making rather funny comments.

Then it happened. There had been a week of bad weather and none of us had been on the beach. I was sitting on the pier wondering when the rain would ease up when I found Carmen standing there, eyes sparkling.

"I'm married!" she said.

For a while I couldn't speak. I'd swallowed my lump of toffee. When the pain in my chest had diminished I lifted one earpiece of my bathing hat so as not to miss a word and wished her and Guy a lifetime of bliss.

"Not Guy," she said. "Toothy. I'm Mrs Gordon!"

"But . . ." I said, which wasn't much help but it was all I could think of to say in the stress of the moment.

"Be a sweet and tell Guy for me, will you? It'll be easier coming from you." And with a wifely peck on my cheek she was gone.

I found Guy in the sail-locker, darning a sail.

"Er, Guy, er," I said. "Er, Carmen's married. Asked me to tell you. Married Toothy. She's Mrs Gordon."

Guy stared at me with his unblinking, mariner's gaze.

"They're married," I repeated. "Married. Wed. Mr and Mrs Gordon."

Still no response.

"Miss Rowbottom has joined Mr Gordon in Holy Matrimony . . ."

As I ploughed on a horrifying truth dawned upon me. The splendid Guy, my idol, was as thick as a post. As dim as a nun's nightlight.

"Your ex-girl-friend and the man with few teeth are as one . . ."

But nothing was registering. As I sweated on, trying to get the message home to him, the scales dropping from my eyes like autumn leaves in a gale, I realised that My Hero was a man of few words because he only knew a few. In fact, apart from a few everyday phrases like 'Pass the marmalade', and 'Does this train stop at Faversham?' his entire vocabulary was nautical.

And so I translated my message into the language he knew.

"Mr Gordon and Miss Rowbottom," I said, "have sailed together into the harbour of matrimony. And are moored together for life."

Immediately he understood. His figure sagged. He seemed to be trying to say something.

I stood with him, but my words of comfort were of no use.

At dawn the following morning a longshoreman, out early to dig bait and nick things from the bathing huts, found Guy as I had left him; staring into space and muttering over and over again the harsh truth which he had, somehow, to accept:

"Carmen . . . Toothy Gordon . . . Moored!"

The game is not worth the candle

Proverb

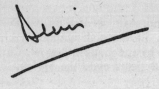

Continuing our series, Cameos Of The Great Composers, the spotlight falls today on George Frederick Handel, the man who cleffed such great musicals as *Acis and Galatea,* both of which must be familiar to all lovers of the semi-classics.

Born in Germany, Handel acquired, according to the *Oxford Dictionary of Music*, 'a great reputation as a keyboard performer', a statement which we can only hope means he played the piano. After a spell as Kapellmeister to the Elector of Hanover, a dying craft nowadays, he came to England and took up residence just outside Edgware in 1710. At least we believe that to have been his room-number but many pages of the parish-records were torn out in the Great Plague, there being no cleaning-tissues in those days.

However, the composer was immediately made welcome by the Edgware gentry, for even in those days Handel was a name which opens all doors. As a young bachelor with several concerti grossi under his belt, to say nothing of his Harmonious Blacksmith, he was especially courted by parents of unmarried daughters and it was in this connection that he was accosted one day by Sir Tenleigh Knott.

Sir Tenleigh, a member of the old nobility, was the sixth son of the seventh Earl - or it may have been the seventh son of the sixth Earl, it was very difficult to tell with all those winding staircases - and he possessed an unmarried daughter, Arabella. She was a vivacious girl, not pretty by any accepted standards, if anything ugly by any accepted standards, but she could speak Latin and foot a quadrille and sometimes the two simultaneously if the tempo was right. So it was of her that Sir Tenleigh bethought himself when he espied Handel by the Long Meadow, for in those days Edgware was all fields even the agricultural land.

"Ah," said Sir Tenleigh, greeting him boisterously, "George Frederick Handel, isn't it?"

"Isn't it what?" said Handel, betraying his Teutonic meticulousness.

"Isn't it a shame that a nice young fellow like you should still be unmarried," said Sir Tenleigh, who never believed in shilly-shallying. "It's unnatural, that's what it is. I'll wager that since you arrived in this country, the only thing you've taken out is your naturalisation papers."

The remark contained enough truth to give Handel pause. Only too well did he know the torments of the flesh, having been up all the previous night with indigestion, a consequence of researching 'Alexander's Feast'. A wife who might be as adept at cooking as she was fair and slim of limb was a prospect which appealed to him strongly. So, "You have maybe somebody in mind?" he asked.

"My daughter Arabella," came the elder man's prompt reply. "An extremely vivacious girl. Gay, jolly, you might even say sporty."

"What does she look like?"

It was the age of 'arranged' marriages, as distinct from today's 'untidy' ones, so it was no unusual thing for two young people to be wed without ever having seen each other before the ceremony. Nevertheless, "What does she look like?" Handel asked.

"Foots a quadrille while speaking perfect Latin,"

said old Sir Tenleigh. "You have made a wise choice."

"What does she look like?"

"How's the *Messiah* going? Finished the Honolulu Chorus yet?"

"What does she look like?"

"Tell you what I'm prepared to do," Sir Tenleigh said. "I am willing to settle an estate on her." The truth was, Arabella had a shape it was perfectly possible to settle an estate on. Her main drawback had always been her resemblance to an early Georgian road-block but it was not a factor Sir Tenleigh felt like discussing.

"What does she look like?" enquired Handel again.

"You have made an old man very happy," said Sir Tenleigh, shaking his hand warmly. "Welcome to the Knott family."

"What does she look like?" Handel called after his departing figure, receiving in reply a cheery wave.

It was a troubled George Frederick who sat that night weighing up half a pound of toccatas. Somewhere deep within him he felt the vague unease that sometimes besets a man when he realises he's marrying a woman he's never laid eyes on. On impulse, he called in his manservant, a devoted local rustic named Walter, to whom the composer later dedicated his chart-topping *Handel's Walter Music*. "I want you should run an errand for me," Handel said tossing him a florin, and we must remember that in those days a florin was worth - what? Two shillings, at least. "Go take a look at Miss Arabella Knott."

"'Ow will oi know 'er?" enquired Walter.

"She'll be the one footing a quadrille in Latin, very gay with it."

"What do 'ee want to know about 'er?" asked the rustic.

"What does she look like?"

When Walter returned, Handel could hardly wait to get the details, having by this time got himself worked up into a right state. "Tell me," he demanded eagerly, "Was she tall and fair, the vivacious Arabella? Was she a delicate wand of beauty? Was she straight as a yew-tree, slim as far-off violins?"

The rustic, in his slow way, sighed. What was the gentlest way he could break the news of Arabella's dimensions to this quivering Hun? Perhaps the only course was to be blunt. "Oi be sorry," he replied -

"The gay Miss Knott were thick, Handel."

There is no fire without some smoke

Proverb

Frank

There has been a fatality in the village. The taped music in the Saloon Bar of the 'Red Lion' was switched off for twenty-four hours as a mark of respect, Mrs Dean removed the prop from her clothes-line and flew her washing at half-mast, Mrs Macnamara wore a black band on her sleeve but as her coat was also black nobody noticed, and the village schoolchildren, on a nature ramble, punched each other in a muted fashion, as though their hearts weren't in it.

Philomel, the donkey, has passed away, and the opening ceremony of the Thorpe Grand Autumn Fair Admission Free All Proceeds to Village Charities will never be the same. Never again will Mr Johns, the chairman, say "Ladies and Gentleman, it gives me great pleasure to declare this year's Thorpe Grand Autumn Fair open . . ." only to be interrupted by a window-rattling bray and the entrance of Philomel. She would pause in front of the platform, paw the ground twice, roll an eye, and then sink onto her front elbows and waggle her tail at Mr Johns. One year she pawed the floor three times and forgot to roll her eye; several children burst into tears and there was a very stiff letter indeed in the following Thursday's local paper. Philomel's annual appearance had to be exactly the same

175

each year. Young men would emigrate from Thorpe to Australia, marry, and return to Thorpe confident that their offspring, would witness exactly the same ceremony that they had witnessed as ladlings. Philomel represented tradition, and continuity.

Mr Johns' eye was moist at the Parish Council meeting last night. "It wouldn't be a Thorpe Grand Autumn Fair without Philomel, me dears," he said. He was right too.

It wasn't really much of a Grand Fair *with* Philomel. Thorpe Village hall is on the small side and only accommodates a few stalls. First came the games. There was the popular bucket-of-water-with-a-sixpence-in-the-bottom; the idea being to drop pennies into the water in the wistful hope that one would cover the sixpence and win a small prize. The trouble with that game was that since inflation and decimalisation one had to drop a 2p piece and attempt to cover a 10p piece, which is larger than a 2p piece.

Next came a game of rolling rubber balls down an inclined plane in an attempt to get them into holes. Unhappily the board had warped over the years and however you rolled the balls they all ended up in the bottom left-hand corner.

The most popular item came next; a stiff, wriggly wire along which you were supposed to pass a brass curtain-ring. The thing was wired up so that if your hand trembled a bell rang. The wires were still there but the old-fashioned battery had become obsolete fifteen years ago so the bell did not ring and everybody won a prize.

Then there was the cake stall. The home-made cakes were so popular that they were all bought by the stall-holders before the Fair opened.

And finally there was the ever-popular Jumble stall. For the last twenty years this has consisted of a slightly rusty golf-club with the string unwinding from the handle, the sole survivor of a pair of book-ends, a pottery biscuit barrel with the knob missing from the lid and the brass showing through the chromium, a glass 'snow-storm'

176

paper-weight with the Eiffel Tower inside which you turned upside down and nothing happened, a pianola roll of 'Marche Militaire', and four books: *Hiawatha, Rendered into Latin*, F. W. Newman, 1862; *Our Debt and Duty to the Soil, The Poetry and Philosophy of Sewage Utilisation*, E. D. Girdlestone, 1878; *Little Elsie's Book of Bible Animals*, 1878; and *Hindustani Self-Taught by the Natural Method*, E. Marlborough, 1908.

When I first came to the village I did not understand how these fêtes and fairs worked. I bought the biscuit barrel and kept it for tobacco. I was quietly corrected by the energetic lady who collected all the jumble for the various functions, Mrs Rumbold.

"If you don't mind me pointing out," she said, "these items are for buying and handing back, not for keeping. What you do is give the biscuit barrel back to me and it comes up at the Church Christmas Bazaar. I then collect it for the Scouts Hut Fund Jamboree. After that it goes to the Young Wives' Bring-and-Buy, the Annual Village Fête, the Darby and Joan White Elephant Night, the Thorpe Dramatic Society Bargain Sale, and it then ends up again at the Thorpe Grand Autumn Fair. It brings in sixpence a time. If you hang on to it, Mr Muir, you are depriving village charities of three shillings and sixpence per annum."

My cheek mantling, I handed the biscuit barrel to Mrs Rumbold to be put back into circulation.

So you see the Grand Autumn Fair could hardly be described as a riveting, compulsive, not-to-be-missed-at-any-cost event. Except for Philomel.

"How did she . . . ?" I asked Mr Johns.

"Internal trouble." he said, quietly. "Sam is heart-broken."

Sam Thornton, the ancient old jobbing gardener, was not only Philomel's owner, he was also her front legs. Her back legs were occupied by Sam's brother Ron. Twenty years ago Ron had been lifting some leeks when his back clicked and he found that he had locked at right angles. He soon got used to walking about with his back at ninety degrees to his legs and Sam, being community minded, decided to make use of Ron's affliction for the good of charity and make him the back half of a pantomime donkey. Sam got the lady on the green who does bespoke loose covers for sofas to make the body out of canvas, Mr Hyde, the Egham saddler, made leather hooves and a papier-mâché head - and Philomel was born. Sam loved his moment of glory. Every first of September he would rub his hands and say, "Come on Ron, time to get the old moke working!" And they would practise for weeks.

"Last week," said Mr Johns. "Ron accidently backed into a pitchfork and straightened up for the first time in twenty years. Trouble was, though, he locked upright. Couldn't bend an inch. Sam had to find somebody else to work the back half. Do you know his great-nephew Fred?"

"City lad from Staines?" I said. "Bit thick? Keeps putting his skid-lid on back to front and riding into walls?"

"That's him. Well, Sam has been training him up to be the back legs. Last night Sam was giving him an extra hour's waggling practice when the lad suddenly went quiet. The next thing Sam knew was a terrible pain, a searing agony in his behind. He couldn't help leaping forward. The old, half-perished canvas ripped, and poor old Philomel was torn in half."

"But why the pain? What . . . ?"

"Fred had lit up a cigarette. The old boy couldn't bear to cope with Philomel's remains so I took her to the road-sweeper, who was cleaning the drain by the bus-stop, and . . . I had her put down."

To break the long silence I said, "Well, I suppose we go ahead anyway with getting the jumble together and getting the cakes baked. . . ?"

"No," said Mr Johns. And he put into words what we, and the whole village, knew to be a sad but real truth:

"There is no Fair without Sam's moke."

178

'Old Father Thames'

Title of Song

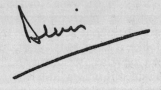

"Mr Norden," said this temporary shorthand-typist. "One more criticism about my spelling and I shall resign. You hear me? R-E-Z-Y-N, resign!"

Once again I silently maligned Brenda's husband. Brenda is my real secretary, the permanent one. A dear sweet girl, she's been with me for fifteen years, never a word of complaint, always unerringly efficient. Then, last year, she had the unmitigated gall to go and get married. And it was while she was away on her honeymoon - three whole days if you don't mind! - that I was forced to acquaint myself with that phenomenon of modern office life, the temporary secretary. Or, as they advertise themselves, 'Temps'.

For those of you who may be still unfamiliar with this consciousness-lowering group, let me explain their significance. You know how God dictated the Ten Commandments to Moses? Well if, instead of Moses, he had dictated them to a Temp - we would now all be working on only Four Commandments. Temps come in every size and shape but there are three characteristics shared by all of them: the first is a total unfamiliarity with the language the British use when communicating with each other, the second is the most tenuous acquaintanceship with the skills of shorthand and typing, the third is extremely little between the ear-rings.

I well remember the first one who came in to give a helping hand, at a hire-charge of 75p per hour per finger. Brenda was going off on another pleasure jaunt, some frivolity connected with a burst appendix, so I phoned the Agency to send over a temporary typist. What turned up was a lanky creature who, with her platform shoes and metal hair rollers, appeared to be about seven foot tall. Looking for all the world like a sexy radar-mast, she marched straight over to the typewriter, sat down and hit some keys. "Oh, look," she said. "It makes little letters."

When the next one arrived, I was somewhat cagier. "Before you start," I said, "Could you tell me your speeds?"

"Well, I'm afraid I only do thirty words a minute," she said.

"Is that shorthand or typing?"

"No," she said, "reading."

To list all the agonies I have endured would be as boring for you as they were painful to me. On one occasion I went into Brenda's office to see how a short fat Temp was getting on with typing one of my letters, because when I'd dictated it to her she'd interrupted to ask how to spell comma. I found her sitting at the desk using two typewriters simultaneously; one with the left hand, the other with the right hand. Noticing my stupefaction, she gave a nervous smile. "I'm sorry," she said, "I couldn't find any carbon paper."

"How are you on the switchboard?" I asked one who'd pitched up looking like an explosion in a remnants factory. "Dunno," she replied. "I never done it on there." I remember the girl who arrived four hours late, having got out of the lift one floor down and spent the whole morning working for the wrong firm; the one who tried to look up telephone numbers in the *Oxford Dictionary*; the one who insisted on having a manual typewriter but an electric eraser. I had one girl who took snuff and another whose only previous commercial experience had been as a commère in a Dolphinarium.

I don't know what qualifications the Agencies require from a girl before they send her out. My private belief is that they show each applicant a washing-machine, a refrigerator and a typewriter. If she can identify the typewriter, she's on the books. What I know for certain is that ever since Brenda's perfidy forced me into availing myself of these creatures, I am become but a Xerox of my former self. Last week I asked one of them if she would fetch me a book of synonyms. "Oh, I love his books," she said. "Specially the Maigrets."

The breaking point came this morning. A new Temp had arrived - the usual type, dolled up to the nines and trailing glories of cloudiness. After I had dictated my first letter to her, I said cautiously, "Do you think you could read it to me back, please?"

"Beg pardon?"

"Please read it to me back."

You won't believe this. That girl got up and started to *walk round behind me.* . . .

That's when I cried 'enough'. "No more temporary secretaries until further notice!" I screamed down the phone to the Agency.

It was only when the twitching ceased that it occurred to me that there might have been a more succinct way of putting the request. Musically. The way Peter Dawson used to sing it -

"Hold Further Temps!"

'Maybe It's Because I'm A Londoner'

Hubert Gregg
Title of Song

Frank

I'm retired now, of course. I retired about, oooh, no it was before that. I retired twice, as a matter of fact. For many years I worked for the General Post Office. I was employed at the Charing Cross Road, London, branch to stand behind a window and say, "I'm sorry but this window is closed, try the next one up". But when I retired from that my sister made me take another job for a week and retire again, because she didn't fancy having a brother who was a retired postal worker, in however responsible a position. That is the sister who was on the stage but is now in Dorking. She married, you know. Quite a few times. If my memory does not play me false, she is now married, or was at the time of her last Christmas card, to a gentleman who processes the films for a photographer attached to a local estate agency. She always refers to him as 'my husband the Property Developer'. So to please her I took a job at a garage for a week, coiling up the air-line used for inflating tyres, and then retired again. She always refers to me as 'my brother the retired Air-Line Executive'.

I am quite happy in my little room, not a stone's throw from Notting Hill. It is what is called a Bed-Sit. That is to say, if you want to sit you have to sit on the bed. I've lived in this same room for, it must be, oooh, or was it the year that, um. . . .

Until I found my little friend, my pet, I became rather lonely. I had my music, of course. I hum a great deal when I am on my own, sometimes accompanying myself on an old bongo drum which the previous tenant used for storing dried melon seeds. It is, I suppose, a humdrum existence, but there we are.

Ah. I was telling you of my pet. Well, I became lonely when I found it increasingly difficult to move about either swiftly or for any length of time. I am on the ninth floor and I soon found that although I could get down the stairs without difficulty I only had enough energy left to get back up again, with none to spare for going out. I had a friend, a Miss Winstanley, who lived in the basement. She was for many years Miss-On-Cash in a Mayfair butcher's shop until she retired some, oooh, it must now, let me see. . . . Well, we came to an arrangement whereby we met halfway down, or in her case halfway up, the stairs. There we would chat, d'you see, of the weather and similar topics, and we would return to our own rooms in fair condition, having divided the expenditure of energy between us.

But after a year or so we both began to feel less capable of tackling the stairs. It was all right when we each managed three flights, we could lean over the banisters and shout to each other. However, we soon could only manage two flights each and as neither of us could see or hear the other, with five flights of stairs in between, there seemed little point in continuing the arrangement.

That was when I began to feel lonely. Unhappily dogs and cats were strictly forbidden in the house. Rather surprising, really, because the landlord, Mr Carew-Entwistle-Carew, is clearly a dog-lover; he always arrives to collect the rent with two Doberman pinschers.

Then one day the problem was solved for me. I did not find myself a pet; a pet found me.

It was a bee. A handsome, brown bee. He was so plump and had such a rich fur coat that I christened him

Diaghilev. I presume he must have fallen from a hive that was being transported through London on the back of a lorry because he was obviously lost and quite grateful to have somewhere to rest his head. I made him a little nest in the bongo drum and he took to staying with me all night and most of the day, buzzing off occasionally when he felt like it. He was free to come and go as he pleased; if the window was shut he could always fly out through the hole in the ceiling where the slate blew off in 1961, or through the aperture in the wall where I rather imagine a wash-basin used to be.

Diaghilev and I got along splendidly for some weeks but then he began to lose weight. As the days sped past he became thinner and thinner until he no longer looked like a ballet impresario but more like the last half-inch of a used pipe-cleaner. I was in despair, as you might well imagine. And then I realised the problem was simply food. Bees eat nectar, and Diaghilev must have buzzed himself half silly trying to find nectar in Notting Hill.

I sprang, at my own pace, into action. I coerced my nice Health Visitor to bring me up a bucket of soil and a selection of honeysuckle plants. These I put into an old, oblong wooden box, which I had used for many years to hold my boot-cleaning things. This I fixed on my, albeit crumbling, window-ledge. I watered the plants with great care, and they flourished.

Oh, the joy of watching Diaghilev restore himself to health! I could not see the expression on his little face as he dipped, soared, buzzed, and then settled over the honey-suckle flowers - my eyes are not what they were - but I am sure that he wore a happy look. In a few days he filled out and became his old, sleek self again.

My cup of happiness became full a week later. He found himself a girl friend, a smaller, even sleeker bee, whom he brought home to show off his window box. And quite suddenly one morning I noticed that Diaghilev was buzzing a different buzz, a high-pitched, interrupted buzz. He was engaged!

Every now and then somebody comes on the wireless and talks about bee-keeping, and they always say that you can't keep bees in a city, that to keep bees you need to own land so that they can have acres of fields and flowers to feed on. I just smile, and look at fat, happy Diaghilev buzzing round my window-box, and I hum a little hum to myself. I hum -

'My bee eats because I'm a landowner!'

A rose is a rose is a rose

Gertrude Stein
'Sacred Emily'

How strange! How really very strange! Do you know, that's the second time today I've come across that line. Isn't that a coincidence? No, really, sometimes I go for weeks without encountering 'a rose is a rose is a rose' but today - twice! Small world. This very morning I saw it written down on a note-pad at my psychiatrist's.

Did I tell you I've got this new psychiatrist now? Well, I never really had the confidence in that other fellow. I mean how much confidence can you have in a man who tries to cure a somatic anxiety-depressive psychosis with an ointment? Oh yes, very distinguished-looking, I admit, but that day I came in and heard him saying into the telephone, "Mummy, you'll just have to face up to it, I'm moving into my own flat" - well, that was it. "I'm sorry," I said, "but I must ask you for my symptoms back."

This new man now, what a difference! Don't go asking me whether he's the Jungian school or the Adlerian school because I can't tell you, all I know is it's the one that costs seven guineas a visit, but where the confidence-inspiring is concerned - chalk and cheese. And it's more than just the fact of no longer having to go through the barber's shop to get to him, it's his methods.

Dreams, you see. That's his thing. "I do tend to go a

bundle on dreams," he told me when I signed on with him. So what I have to do now is, I have to keep some paper on the bedside-table and whenever I have a dream, get down a description of it the moment I wake up. Mind you, she leads off a bit about it, the Madam, because of the noise of the typewriter in the middle of the night. But the psychiatrist says take no mind of that, all women are troublemakers, he says, the Greeks had the right idea. Then twice a week I go along to him, lie down on his couch, a rexine one it is and he says the small change that slips down the sides, that's where the real money in psychiatry lies, and after I've read out my dreams to him he interprets them.

Which I must say is more than I could ever do. Just rubbish most of them seem to me, not to mention downright suggestive sometimes. Take the one I was telling him about this morning, the one where I was in a Cowboys and Indians scene. Now I agree that's one I do dream a lot but I've always put it down to childhood, because what with all those Randolph Scott pictures us kids used to go and see up the Regal, we were always playing Cowboys and Indians games. Not that I was ever allowed to be a Cowboy or an Indian in those games, that was always for the stronger boys. Me being so delicate, and like better dressed, I always used to be the lady having a baby in the end waggon.

But it stays in your unconscious, doesn't it, there's no denying it, so in this dream I was telling the psychiatrist about, I was in a waggon-train going along the prairie when suddenly thump-thump-thump, a storm of arrows on the roof. Comanches!

Up gallops the Waggon-master, and I remember something else now, should have told the psychiatrist this, in our games the Waggon-master was always the strongest fighter in the gang, so up gallops Alice, with arrows sticking out all over her, and she shouts, "Get the waggons in a circle."

Now you know how it is with dreams. Immediately she

187

said the words "in a circle" there I was travelling on the Inner Circle. If you don't know what the Inner Circle is, it's part of the London Underground, a transport system which enables you to travel from say Liverpool Street to Blackfriars very much quicker than if you tried to get there crawling on your hands and knees. Anyway, there I was on the Inner Circle and I was stark naked.

"Symbolic," the psychiatrist said when I said that to him.

"All right," I said, "I was symbolic naked." Come to think of it, it's funny really how many of my dreams I do seem to wind up stark symbolic naked. When I'm not having a baby that is. But, as I say, I was travelling naked on the Inner Circle and while I was trying to remember where I could have put my ticket, suddenly the train stops at a station, I look out the window from idle curiosity and what do I see? It's Harrow.

And now it happens again. The moment I see the word 'Harrow', just as suddenly as last time - I'm the Headmaster of Harrow School. May I go blind, the Headmaster of Harrow School. Mortarboard, cane and full sidewhiskers. Otherwise stark naked, of course. And there, bending over in front of me, in a school cap and short trousers, is the psychiatrist. "Stop blubbing, boy," I hear myself saying, "you're down for six of the best."

Now when I got to this bit, the old psychiatrist perked up no end. He stopped shaving, put his electric razor down and came and sat down right there on the couch with me. "And did you cane me?" he says, nibbling his lip. "Talk slower."

Well, as it happens, I didn't cane him. Because, in the dream, just as I raise the cane, I notice he's got something knobbly tucked down the back of his trousers, so I stop. "Whatever you've got down there, boy," I say to him, "fetch it out." So he reaches behind into the seat of his trousers and know what he pulls out? A bust of Cicero. Now how I recognise it's a bust of Cicero is because he's got one himself in his surgery, the psychiatrist, and he showed me it one day. He's got lots of Greek statues round his walls come to think of it, though they're mainly of young fellows carrying wine-cups.

Anyway, in the dream, after he's pulled out the bust of Cicero, I say to him, "Sure there's nothing else down there, lad?" and he sobs "Yes, sir." And from the same place he pulls out another bust of Cicero. Then another one, then another one.

And from then on, the sort of nightmare-thing sets in, because he keeps on pulling them out. One bust of Cicero after another, thirty of them, forty of them. And just when the whole room is getting waist-deep in busts of Cicero - I wake up.

Now, I ask you, what would you have made of a dream like that? Going from a Comanche Indian Raid, to Harrow Station on the Inner Circle, to God knows how many busts of Cicero - wouldn't you say just a lot of old nonsense? No logic in it all?

Me too. But that's why I've got the confidence in this new man. With his college-training, what he deduced right away was that I was revolting. And what was I revolting against? Some old bird called Gertrude Stein. Because, showing me the three little notes he'd made on his note-pad, he said what they represented was my unconscious rejection of Gertrude Stein.

What he'd written, you see, was -

"Arrows . . . sees Harrow . . . Ciceros."

Allons, enfants de la patrie!

Rouget de Lisle
'La Marseillaise'

Frank

I had this nasty experience with a pair of trousers.

For years I bought my trousers from the same shop, a dimly lit, mahogany-panelled oasis of calm in an alley off Bond Street. Mr Herring, who was about a hundred and four, would creep forward, fingering the tape measure round his neck, and ask my pleasure. Having selected a likely pair of trousers I would be waved into the Changing Cabinet to try them on. The Changing Cabinet was about the size of an average hotel bedroom and it always contained Mr Herring's partner, Mr Butterfield, furtively eating egg sandwiches. Mr Butterfield, who was about a hundred and six, would mumble apologies and back out, shedding crumbs, and I would examine myself in a spotted pier-glass while Mr Herring fussed round me ensuring that the trousers fitted snugly under the arm-pits and that there was plenty of room in the seat for sitting.

When I went back there a few months ago the shop had gone. In its place was a shop selling Japanese cameras and coloured slides of the Changing of the Guard, so I had, perforce, to find another seller of trousers. It's all changed, hasn't it? Whereas I once dealt with Herring, Butterfield and Nephew (Estd. 1901), I found myself entering a shop called the Kensington Panty Boo-Teak.

And there was no Changing Cabinet. When it came to trying on the trousers I was shown a row of booths up against the wall. These had no door, as such, just a pair of extremely inadequate cowboy saloon swing doors, about eighteen inches deep, hung half-way up.

I don't know what the height of the normal trouser tryer-onner is but I don't think that it is six feet six inches, which is what I am. The vulnerable area was in grave danger; indeed, had I been wearing unduly thick socks I would probably have been arrested. But worse was to follow. It was impossible, I found, to remove one pair of trousers and encase the legs in a trendy new pair whilst standing bolt upright. A certain amount of knee-bending was unavoidable. It was while I was doubled over in a kind of foetal crouch trying to get my feet into the new trousers that I found myself gazing into the eyes of a lady sitting on a couch opposite. The full horror then dawned. Not only was any kind of privacy impossible but it was a mixed establishment open to both sexes. I shouted for an assistant, because the trousers, by an error of manufacture, appeared to have the zip at the back, to be faced by a ravishing Deb-of-the-Year who promptly burst into squeals of laughter and shrieked to the whole shop that I'd put my trousers on back to front.

I staggered out of the booth feeling very wobbly indeed. All I wanted was a sit-down for a few minutes. I sagged into a seat and closed my eyes. Almost immediately I heard a male voice say, "You look a bit ribby, squire. Permit me to do the laying on of the hands."

I opened my eyes to see an odd figure looming over me. He was wearing a wide, black sombrero, and a cloak of some dark material, underneath which was a bus conductor's uniform.

"Hold still, guv," he said. He put his fingers on my head, kneaded the scalp a bit, and hummed the opening bars of 'La Marseillaise'.

"Ta-tum, ti-tum, tum, ta, ti, TA, ti-tum . . . Feeling better now?"

"No," I said. "Exactly as before."

"Blast!" he said "It's no go, I'm afraid. Oh, well, it was worth trying."

He joined me on the seat and handed me a card. It read 'Alonzo Rathbone. Layer-On Of Hands. Cures While-U-Wait.'

"But," I said, "you're a bus conductor."

"Professionally I conduct buses, that is true." he said. "But by vocation, I am a Healer."

"Of people?"

"Well, no. That's the problem. So far, only plants. I was hoping for a breakthrough with you, but alas, it was not meant. My Granny's glad."

"What about?"

"No, no," he said. "Her glad. Her gladioli. That's how I discovered I had this gift. The gladioli were wilting and I was touching them, fondling them, and I began to hum the opening bars of the Marseillaise, and suddenly my fingertips went all trembly and I could feel a kind of energy leaving me and entering into the glad. Next day the glad was so sprightly that Gran entered it in the Stoke Newington Darby and Joan flower show and won a linen tea-towel with a recipe for bouillabaisse printed on it. Sorry I couldn't help you, guv, but if you ever have trouble with wilting plants, fruit trees, leguminous veg, just get in touch with me. Remember the name, Alonzo Rathbone." And with a swing of his cloak he strode off to the bus depot.

I forgot all about Alonzo until a few days ago. I don't know about you but we have had a disastrous year in the garden. The front gate got Dutch Elm Disease; the white paint turned yellow and the top bar crumbled away. The new rose bed was too near the oil central heating chimney and all the roses went down with flue. The lawn stopped growing, went brown, and still had a new mown look after seven weeks; a classic case of newmownia. But worst of all our Comice pear-tree had a nervous breakdown.

"Look at it!" said my wife, her face twisted with grief.

"Our oldest tree! Our delight! And now - brown leaves, bark flaking away. And look at the pears! They look more like spotty nutmegs!"

It certainly looked a goner.

"My favourite tree in the whole garden. The whole world," said my wife, plying the hanky. "Doomed. Nobody can save it now!"

"Alonzo!" I yelled, without warning.

"What?"

"There is just a chance in a million that I know a man who could restore it to health. With his 'fluence. He touches them up!"

I hurtled upstairs and found the trousers I had bought at the Boo-Teak. I had never worn them because when I got them home they seemed to have been designed for a seventeen year old, colour-blind neuter, but inside the hip pocket was the card I was looking for, reading 'Alonzo Rathbone. Layer-On Of Hands. Cures While-U-Wait'. But - oh, misery - no address.

But you never know your luck. Perhaps bus conductors read books like this to while away the time between rush hours. If so I have a message for a Mr Rathbone. More than a message, really, a plea to make two middle-aged fruit fanciers happy:

"Alonzo, fondle our pear-tree!"

Sweet are the uses of adversity

William Shakespeare
'As You Like It'

In a previous book of 'My Word!' stories (*A finger on the pulse of our time. . . F. Muir*), I made mention of Mrs Thora Tidmarsh, our local High Priestess where cultural matters are concerned. Mrs Tidmarsh is a strapping clear-eyed lady, well-built without being the slightest bit sexy, like a Junior Minister's wife, and if Concorde had been able to develop the same amount of thrust it would now be plying the Atlantic. As is often the way with such ladies, her husband Arthur, although an extremely good credit-risk, is so totally devoid of personality he gives the impression he'd come out black and white even on colour TV. At the soirées which established his wife's ascendancy as local arbiter on all questions artistic, her Sunday Afternoon Musical Teas, he was little more than a plate-passer.

Those Sunday afternoons were occasions of absolutely teeth-aching refinement. They took place in her lovely dining-room, a muted mixture of all the more expensive greens and browns but furnished with so many marble-top tables it was like eating in an indoor cemetery. While you munched hopelessly at unidentifiable squares of thin bread, Mrs Tidmarsh played - and thoroughly explained - records of what is called 'atonal' music. It is called that, I most sincerely hope, because somebody, sometime, is going to have to atone for it. Of the whole experience, what I remember most clearly is that peculiar ache in the neck one only gets from too much nodding appreciatively.

However, because the presence of every person invited was unfailingly reported in the local press, Mrs Tidmarsh's Musical Teas became a sort of social Access Card. If the Manager of the Supermarket had noticed your name among the list of those attending, his man at the check-out could be persuaded to help hump your shopping out to the car. For that reason no-one ever turned down an invite and Mrs Tidmarsh reigned unchallenged as cultural champ of N.W.11.

Unchallenged, that is, until the arrival in the neighbourhood of Alf and Rowena Hughes. The first hint that these two might qualify as contenders for the title came from the milkman, our quartier's acknowledged William Hickey. "Hey," he said, "know them new people who've taken Number Seventy-Four? They're installing one of them libidos in their bathroom."

It was - insofar as such an item can be so designated - a straw in the wind. Our suspicions that the Hugheses might prove persons of social consequence were strengthened when the local paper printed a story that Rowena intended to stage a Women's Liberation protest demonstration at the next Hampstead Heath Bank Holiday Fair. "I intend to lead a march," she was reported as saying, "demanding the abolition of Halfway For Ladies at the coconut-shy."

The actual gauntlet was thrown down in the form of a startling handwritten invitation stuffed into all our letter-boxes. Startling, I mean, by Tidmarsh literary standards. "Hi, new neighbours!" it read, in day-glo colours, "It's getting-to-know-ya-time! Why not mosey up the trail to the Hughes ranch 4 pm this Sunday? Strong drink, light nosh and Poetry Reading!"

Poetry Reading! Well, I can tell you, the Washeteria that Saturday was a veritable buzz of indecision and in the Supermarket there was a five-cart pile-up. Was Sunday to be the Hugheses or the Tidmarshes? On the credit side, the milkman's last broadcast had stated that the Hughes's drawing room contained an ozone-spraying humidifier and inflatable Queen Anne chairs. On the debit side, might not the exchange of explained-music for spoken-poetry turn out to be a frying-pan and fire situation?

"Depends what kind of poetry it is," said the man from Number Sixteen, who runs a boutique called Mad Togs For Englishmen. "Like, T. S. Eliot like, he's quite catchy. My Mum had a record of him doing 'I Used To Sigh For The Silvery Moon', you could get the hang of it practically first go off."

"Could we perhaps ring and *ask* them what kind of poetry?" offered Mr Twenty-Eight, who manufactures pregnant window-dummies for Mothercare. It was a bright suggestion so he was deputed to go and make the phone call.

He came back wearing a rather dazed expression. "Guess what?" he said. "The Golden Treasury of Erotic Verse!"

So that's how Thora Tidmarsh's supremacy was broken, that's how a musical experience was exchanged for a literary experience, that's how wife-swapping got started in Hampstead Garden Suburb.

What often runs through my mind, though, is the phrase that Thora must have used to Arthur on the following Monday morning - after the milkman had arrived to tell her exactly *why* her Sunday afternoon audience had deserted her.

"Sweetheart," she must have said -

"Sweetheart, the Hugheses offer verse at tea."

If at first you don't succeed, try, try again

William Edward Hickson
'Try and Try Again'

Frank

"It is time," said my wife, "that you gave the puppy a bath."

A simple, friendly, wifely statement, spoken in a gentle, well-modulated tone, and yet my innards twisted into a knot. What was an undeniable truth was that Lady Ottoline Morrell - for that was our Afghan hound puppy's name - was, at the age of fifteen months, a bit old to be called a puppy, and was very long overdue for her first bath. As the condition of our house bore witness.

To begin with, the phrase 'giving the puppy a bath' conjures up a picture of gently dunking a scrap of fur in a pudding-basin of warm suds. It inadequately describes wrestling desperately with four and a half stone of powerfully-sinewed, wilful, furious doormat. I couldn't get her anywhere near the pudding-basin.

It might well be that high up in the hills of Afghanistan above Kabul a simple old shepherd had only to whistle once through blackened teeth for his obedient hound to round up a herd of alpaca, or cashmere goats, or whatever they rear up there to make those smelly coats out of, before leaping unbidden into a hot bath. But our puppy's mother came from Chelmsford, and the native skills seem to have been bred out of the strain in the soft life of the Home Counties.

If I whistled at Otty to summon her she would stop what she was doing and look at me with a mild surmise. If I whistled again with more authority she would smile gently to herself, tongue lolling out, then lope away before human behaviour became even more eccentric.

And it was hopeless to give chase. Otty could accelerate from rest to thirty mph in five yards and maintain that cruising speed indefinitely. She could go even faster out of doors.

I decided on a policy of stealth; Softly, Softly Wettee Otty. Squeezy tube of dog shampoo in left hand, water-bomb in right (as every schoolboy knows, along with 'who imprisoned Montezuma', a water-bomb is a large plastic bag full of water, which explodes on impact, deluging the victim).

This plan was not wholly successful. In retrospect I think that I was wrong to wear gumboots. These not only slow down the bomber's speed to well below thirty knots but the top of the gumboot acts as a funnel which receives the water when the lolloping action of running causes the plastic bag to rupture.

I changed out of gumboots, put on a dry right sock, and resolved that even though I had, at first, not succeeded I would try again. This time with the garden hose.

I shoved the nozzle of the hose down my shirt and strolled nonchalantly towards Otty, who was lying on the grass trying to hypnotise a sparrow into coming within paw range. She eyed me warily. I walked on right past her and waggled my hips, a sign to my wife in the garage to turn the water on. I removed the nozzle from my shirt and waited for the water to come through so that I could swing suddenly round and, to Otty's astonishment, drench her.

No water came. Not a trickle. I waggled my hips furiously. The hose remained dry. I turned to see what had gone wrong and there was Otty, tongue lolling happily, sitting on the hose.

"Off it!" I shouted. "Giddup! Nice Otty! Here girl! Up!" She made no move.

It was then that I made my mistake. In order to have both hands free to wave at Otty I shoved the nozzle of the hose down my trousers. At which moment Otty got off the hose.

How often can the human spirit try again before despair sets in? As I changed into dry trousers I was on the point of giving up when my eye alighted on a newspaper which had been pressed into service to line a drawer. Facing me was a photograph of a riot in Japan. And pictured there was my answer to the problem of how to give Otty a bath; a water-cannon. A device which could saturate a thousand aggrieved Japanese would surely be capable of dampening Otty.

The ironmongers in Egham did not stock water-cannons, I found, but I was able to borrow from Mrs Caddy a device which worked on exactly the same principle. Mrs Caddy called it a Grain Lifter and she used it on her farm to shift grain from a cart up to the top of her silo. It was a vast machine which plugged into the mains and consisted basically of a pipe which was thrust into the grain which needed to be lifted, an electric blower, and another pipe on top which squirted the grain, under great pressure, in whichever direction she wished it to be squirted.

I planned the operation most carefully. The Grain Lifter was towed in by tractor and parked on the lawn. I plugged it in to a 13 amp. plug in the house. The feed tube was inserted into a barrel of rainwater and the gun end was trained upon a spot, some twenty yards away, where I had assembled a little pile of goodies; old raincoats, telephone directories, chamois leathers, peppermints, elderly eggs, string from the Sunday joint - all Otty's favourite foods. We let Otty out of the house and she made immediately for the pile, reassured herself that there was nobody lurking within harmful range, and lay down contentedly for a good chew. I gave the signal to switch the current on.

What happened next can only be described as a blinding flash. The Grain Lifter burst into flames, the main fuses in the house blew, and the neon signs went dim outside every betting-shop within a ten mile radius of Thorpe, Surrey.

The magistrate's court at Guildford took the view that I was entirely to blame. They went on and on about negligence and I must have known that the machine was not designed to be used with water and that the manufacturers had warned users that the machine would not work when dampness was present, and had I not seen the warning printed on the side of the machine?

I had seen the warning but, without my reading glasses, I had taken it for a motto encouraging perseverance. What was actually written across the thing, in humiliatingly large letters, was:

'IF AT FIRST YOU DON'T SUCK SEED, TRY DRIER GRAIN.'

Wonders will never cease

Sir Henry Bate Dudley
(*Letter to Garrick, 1776*)

As I grow older - a practice I seem to be falling into more
frequently these days - I find myself making increasing use
of the expression 'mark my words'. Never was the
utterance more bandied than in the argument about
installing central heating.

I was against it, and eloquently. "When did our island
people begin to decline as a world power?" I asked.
"When they started living in warm rooms. Take the
Victorians, whose homes were bone-achingly cold. Why
was it they all went out and conquered tropical countries?
Simply to have somewhere they could take their overcoats
off. Mark my words, when we lost our goose-pimples, we
lost our greatness. Moreover" - that's another word I've
taken to, since the prematurely-greys - "moreover, when
central heating came in, do you realise what went out?
Chilblains! One of the greatest losses the hedonists of this
country have ever suffered. Make what claims you will
about your wife-swapping and your hard-core and your
orgies, the permissive society has come up with no pleasure
so purely ecstatic as scratching a chilblain."

I was, as usual, in a minority of one. Despite all my
ingenious rearguard manoeuvres against installation - very
strong peppermints, thermal underwear, letting the baby

sleep in the airing-cupboard - I was eventually forced to yield to domestic pressures. What finally turned the tide against me was when the District Nurse halted at the bird-cage one December day. "Oh," she exclaimed, "what pretty bluebirds!" On learning they were canaries, she immediately finked to the Health Department.

So it was we began the whole dreary business of Heating Engineers and boilers and radiators and British Thermal Units and "you'll have to run the down-pipe through the master bedroom". One of the disadvantages of installing central heating in an aging house is that there is no way of hiding the piping. In consequence, every one of our living areas now gives the appearance of a ship's engine-room.

Let me point out another consequence of adding artificial warmth to a house that has managed to exist without it since before Crippen was apprehended. Everything warps. There is, apparently, a scientific law that heat makes things expand and cold makes them contract - the reason, I suppose, why days are longer in the summer and shorter in the winter. And when it comes to heating houses, this scientific law manifests itself by causing every bit of woodwork to swell, twist, curve and curl.

Doors, for example, jam in the half-open position. That is a peculiarly irritating phenomenon for me because I am a man given to dramatic gestures. In any argument, I have made an extremely satisfying practice of storming out of the room and slamming the door behind me. Now you try doing that with a door that jams in the half-open position. Your arm pulls halfway out of its socket.

Equally irritating, but more financially depressing, is what happens to windows. We have wooden sash-windows and when the central heating was put in, during the summer months, they were all open, in the 'up' position. Around November the wind started making BBC Sound Effect noises so I went round the house pulling down their lower halves. What did I come back with? Fourteen snapped sash-cords. The central heating's trial-run had corrugated every window frame's edge, wedging each one fast within its groove.

"Not to worry," said the carpenter when he called to inspect them. "All it means is supplying and fitting fourteen new window-sections." Then he quoted me a price which could have kept a family of five in the Bahamas for three fun-packed months. "Not on your freelance-writing nelly," said the Bank Manager I went to for the money.

For the rest of the November-to-April period, our rooms, with every window jammed in the open position, presented some fascinatingly varied extremes of temperature. From the new radiators to the middle of the carpet we could have posed for one of those High Speed Gas commercials - everybody smilingly half-dressed and the baby tottering about naked. From the middle of the carpet to the window - Antarctica. On the radiator side of the room, daffodils bloomed. On the window side, edelweiss. The RSPCA said we had the only tortoise with schizophrenia.

I am not an obstinate man. I readily admit that a house without central heating does present certain snags. On a winter's morning it's not always convenient having to run four times round your bedroom before your fingers thaw enough to undo your pyjama buttons. But such a house does possess one important factor in its favour. Mark my words -

"Windows will never seize."

O for the touch of a vanish'd hand

Alfred, Lord Tennyson
'Break, Break, Break'

Frank

It was frightful, standing there in the witness box of the North London Magistrate's Court, looking across at my dear old friend and comrade Denis Norden slumped in the dock.

He seemed drawn, as if by Felix Topolski; and his face looked - as indeed the whole of him had been - pinched. It was only a minor charge on which he stood arraigned, thanks be to merciful Providence; a matter of being caught whistling outside the Golders Green Scottish Presbyterian Church on a Sunday afternoon.

The magistrate was talking to me. "This sort of hooliganism has got to be stamped out. It's the devil's work, d'ye ken?" he said. "But I'm prepared to give the laddie another wee chance. If I bind him over, will you stand surety for his good behaviour? To the tune of five pounds?"

I leapt at the chance of being the instrument of my colleague's freedom.

"Oh yes, sir!" I exclaimed. "Yes, yes! With all my heart! Indeed I will! Oh, yes and yes again!"

"Have you five pounds?"

"And to spare, sir!" I cried.

"Have you five pounds when all your debts are paid?"

A routine little question they always have to ask. Wasting the court's time. It's a wonder they don't do away with it.

"Yes, sir," I answered stoutly. "And I gladly pledge every. . . ."

I paused. I suddenly felt uneasy. Car not a debt - could be whipped back if instalments not paid. Owed Jim Knight the fishmonger for a pair of kippers - but he owed us for a dozen of our eggs so that was a credit rather than a debit. Why this unease?

The mists of memory cleared suddenly. All my debts were most certainly not paid. I had one outstanding debt, years old, and I had no idea how large the amount was.

It must have been about eleven years ago when the debt was incurred. At that time my wife and I had a canal boat, 'SAMANDA', in which we used to potter up and down the Inland Waterways when the summer wasn't too rigorous. I suppose that in a good year we spent about ten days actually afloat in her but we were privileged, as proud owners, to spend every spare hour from September to May scrubbing, derusting, painting and varnishing her so that she wouldn't disintegrate one day when we weren't looking; a trick that boats have.

That summer the drizzle was particularly warm so we decided to take 'SAMANDA' up the Oxford canal and round into the Grand Union, taking in the Blisworth tunnel, which is over a mile and a half long.

Halcyon days they were, with halcyons swooping over the water in a flash of glittering blue.

Occasionally we towed the boat along from the towpath in blissful silence, but we usually used the motor because the tow-rope chafed my wife's neck.

It was all so magical until we got halfway through Blisworth tunnel. Now canal tunnels are pitch dark, moist, and there is just room for two boats to pass. Just.

Half-way through the Blisworth we heard the sound that every Inland Waterway mariner dreads, the thump-thump-thump of an approaching narrow-boat's diesel engine.

Narrow-boats are the old canal working boats, over seventy feet in length, made of steel, or elm planks about a foot thick, and one touch from them can stove in the hull of a fancy little cruiser like ours.

We switched off our engine and clung to the wall on our side of the tunnel, slightly alarmed by a regular series of dull thuds which got louder as the narrow-boat got nearer. When she came into our headlight beam the reason for the thuds became apparent. The narrow-boat was chugging up the tunnel towards us ricocheting from one wall to the other, clearly unmanned.

"It's the 'Flying Dutchman'!" I yelled.

"What, up the Grand Union canal?" replied my wife. "With nobody on board? No, be sensible. If anything it's the 'Marie Celeste'."

In fact, it was the 'Alfred J. Crump'. We found out later that it had been hired by a couple of middle-aged ladies who didn't fancy going through the tunnel so left the engine in gear and hurried over the top to catch the boat at the other end.

By some miracle we were not sunk. The narrow-boat passed by in mid-bounce, but there was a board sticking out of its side which caught our craft a glancing blow at the bows.

"Thank Heavens!" my wife cried. "The only damage is a scratch on the 'AND' of 'SAMANDA'."

"But it's a deep scratch!" I said. "In my lovely varnish-work!"

As soon as we had moored up at the next village I went round asking where I could find a painter who would touch up our boat for us.

I should have known something was wrong when the painter arrived, a most distinguished-looking gentleman with a box of paints, an easel, and an umbrella. He seemed a little surprised when I explained what was wanted but he did a splendid job. It took him about two hours. He used best artist's quality varnish because I sneaked a look at the tin.

When he had finished I pumped his hand enthusiastically and congratulated him on his skill, commanding him to send his bill on to me. We exchanged names.

It was only later, when we were on the homeward leg of our journey, that I glanced at the card he had given me and found that the obliging painter who had touched up our name plate was the President of the Royal Academy.

And his bill has yet to arrive. The mind boggles as to how much two hours of the President of the Royal Academy's time costs. Hundreds? Thousands?

My reverie was broken by the magistrate.

"I asked you whether you have five pounds when your debts are paid!"

"I don't know, sir!" I blurted. "You see, sir, I've just remembered. I have one bill outstanding. So you'd better clap my friend in the clink, sir. You see, sir, I'm afraid I still . . . it's not my fault because he hasn't sent it, but I still . . ."

"You still what, man?"

"Owe for the touch of a varnished 'AND'."

Charity begins at home

Sir Thomas Browne
'Religio Medici'

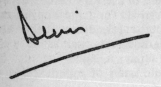

"Among the contributors," read the third paragraph of the letter from the publishing firm, "will be Alexander Solzhenitsyn, Dr Christian Barnard, Lord Hailsham, Mother Teresa and other Television Personalities. The book's title will be *My Most Embarrassing Moment* and we would like its opening chapter to be contributed by you."

When I put the letter down, I could not disguise my pleasure. In addition to the natural gratification I felt at being included among such distinguished company, there was also the knowledge they had picked the right man for the right job. For if my life has been rich in no other ways, where moments of embarrassment are concerned shake hands with a millionaire. The trouble, if anything, was going to be that I had too many to choose from, an embarrassment of embarrassments.

I allowed my mind to wander over some of the more neck-reddening of the incidents. The occasion when a large dog followed me into a telephone box and I couldn't get the door open again? The backstage party given by The London Symphony Orchestra when I decided to slip away unobtrusively and walked right through a harp? The day I took a full-size cactus plant on a crowded Underground train? That moment during the Old Fashioned Waltz with the Lady Mayoress at the Huddersfield Press Ball when I realised that my left-hand contact lens had dropped into her cleavage? The time I spilled a whole cup of hot Bovril into my lap - at a nudist camp?

The mere remembrance of these and similar episodes gave me shudders sufficient to keep my automatic wrist-watch running for three days. However, were any of them, in these particular circumstances, really embarrassing *enough*? For an incident to deserve its place as the opening chapter of that book, surely it must identify itself immediately as an absolute nadir of experience, a true North Finchley of the soul.

Well, as with moments of sex, so with moments of embarrassment: it is often the most recent one that is remembered as the most significant. And as, at that time, my most recent one had happened no more than a month ago - moment of embarrassment, I mean - that was the one I decided to record and submit.

The story started with the fact that, when one of the new take-away shops on the Parade went out of business - there just isn't the demand for organic beefburgers round here - a Japanese gentleman took over the premises and opened it as a Karate Academy. In no time at all he was raking in over a hundred quid a week teaching the neighbouring bourgeoisie how to break planks with their bare hands; to say nothing of the extra tenner or so he knocked up doing a sideline in firewood.

Why was I among the first to enrol? Many reasons, the main one being that having grown up on a cultural diet of those magazines with I Was a Seven Stone Weakling on the inside back cover, I hated acknowledging that, even today, if a bully were to kick sand in my girl's face on the beach I'd probably end up helping him.

The strange thing was, something within me responded to Karate. I was a natural. Within four weeks, Mr Sen informed me that I was probably the best fighting pupil he had, better even than old Mrs Willett. Straightaway I made a silent vow that I would never use my powers for evil, only for good.

I'm going to go into the Historic Present tense now, because it's necessary that the next sequence of events be related as graphically as possible. That night, I'm coming home from the Academy and what do I see? Under a lamp post, two people are struggling. One is a well-built young man, the other a rather frail girl, and he's trying to wrest a handbag from her hands. She is kicking at his shins and struggling, but he's so much bigger than she is there can only be one outcome.

So - Karate-time, folks. In two rapid strides I step between them, raise my right arm and, with the heel of the hand - Hah! Ah! Ha-so! Three beautifully timed strokes, like a cobra, and there he lies - writhing on the ground! The girl gazes at me for a moment, then she seizes my hand and presses it to her soft cheek. Releasing it, she snatches up the handbag and runs off into the night.

Chest swelling, I give the big fellow a nudge with my toe. "On your feet, chummy," I say. "We're going down the nick." He stirs and looks up at me. I notice he has a strangely melting gaze. "Too jolly right we jolly are," he says.

"What do you mean?"

"That was *my* handbag."

Although *My Most Embarrassing Moment* has proved to be a voluminous tome, running to some eight hundred-odd pages, the Editorial Board have unanimously agreed that my contribution fully deserves its position as the opening chapter - a fact which their advertising boys were not slow to pick up. Indeed, it has become the sub-head on most of the publicity releases:

'Karate Begins A Tome.'

What's the good of a home if you are never in it?

George and Weedon Grossmith
'The Diary of a Nobody'

Frank

The other morning at breakfast time I was sitting over a cup of hot coffee when I had a terrific idea. I wasn't even trying to think at the time; I was crouched over the cup trying to steam an egg stain out of the seat of my jeans. If I had a thought in my head at the time it was never again to put a tray with a soft-boiled egg on my chair, move forwards to switch on the television, then back gently and sit down on the egg. If I had been in a thinking mood I might have reflected further on the extraordinary amount of egg there is in an egg; enough in one small oval shell to besmear a cheek and a half of jeans.

But my mind was blank, and into it floated this idea. If pressed for a comparison in the world of nature I would say that it was not at all unlike a mushroom spoor alighting on a damp flannel.

Now every writer dreams about inventing a new character to write novels about. Think how excited Ian Fleming must have been when he dreamed up James Bond, or Galsworthy when he thought of Forsyte Saga. Once a writer has his hero, his Bond or his Saga, the rest is easy; best-sellers, major motion-pictures, television serials.

My idea was a totally original character - a criminal pixie. Or, to put it another way, a bent elf.

For the next three days I put everything else aside and worked like a madman on the plot of the book; I refused all offers of food - except at meal-times, of course - and went without sleep all day, but at the end of it I had a synopsis roughed out.

There are four of them in the gang. Our hero, Norm the Gnome, is the leader. He is a criminal but we make it clear that he is not all that nasty. Nasty-ish but not revolting. He learned his bad habits when he did his National Service - two years in the National Elf Service - and has never since come to terms with society.

Norm's girl-friend is Mustard-Seed, hot stuff, still a bit green, although well past her salad-days. She earns her living as a dancer in the clubs, where she works under her professional name of 'Caustic-Soda'. She is a stripper.

The heavy is Alf the Elf, a huge muscle-bound giant - a giant, that is, up against the elves - who gets all the dirty work to do. He is well known to the police because he unthinkingly allowed himself to be photographed in the nude, rippling his muscles, for the cover of the magazine *Elf and Strength*.

The last member of the group is Puck (real name Robin Badfellow), a layabout who spends most of his time filing his nails and passing remarks. His job with the gang is to act as contact-man and drive the getaway car when they can afford to buy one.

The gang always met on Tuesday evenings because it was a bad night on the telly and one Tuesday Norm strode in very purposefully with a Master Plan.

"Right," he said. "From tonight this gang stops being cat burglars. We've had a good year burgling cats but the market for hot cat-collars even with a bell attached, is satiated. We're going into the big time."

Consternation, as you might well imagine, reigned. The pros and cons were discussed with some heat, but Norm was adamant.

"I'm going to be Mr Big," he said. "Caesar of the Undergrowth. Drive round in an Elfa-Romeo. Take

Mustard-Seed to the South of France, first-class on the Cross-Channel Fairy. So here's what we're gonna do. Next Saturday evening, after the Western on telly, we're going to rob a bank!''

"I know a bank whereon the wild thyme blows,'' said Puck, combing his hair with a thistle.

"That's the one we're going to do!'' said Norm.

"I can't manage Saturday,'' said Puck. "I'll be in the middle of an ice-hockey match.''

"Then Mustard-Seed can be look-out,'' said Norm. "We're going to nick all the thyme from that bank and then take it to a fence.''

"Which Fence?''

"The one at the bottom of my garden. We'll pin it out on the fence to dry, then put it into packets marked 'Dried Herbs' and flog it to Health Food addicts up the Goblin Market. There's a fortune in it.''

"Hey boss,'' said Alf the Elf, to everybody's surprise as he didn't go in much for talking. "We'll get caught. That bank's floodlit!''

Norm silenced him with a look. "We are going to tunnel!'' he announced. "I have recruited Mo the Mole and Harry Hedgehog for the job. We are going to go in underneath the plants and pull them up - *downwards!*''

Everything seemed to be going according to plan on the night. Mo the Mole burrowed a rough tunnel, then Harry the Hedgehog went in and scraped the tunnel smooth with his quills. The roots of the thyme dangled down. Norm dragged the thyme down by its roots and passed it to Alf, who staggered down the tunnel and deposited it in piles outside. And then something went wrong. Alf had disappeared with the last load when Norm had a gnomish feeling that all was not well. He ran down the tunnel to the entrance - and it was blocked. He was trapped by a large clod of turf, which had been rolled over the entrance.

"Somebody has grassed on me!'' he groaned. And sat down to wait for the police.

The story ends with Norm the Gnome staring through

his prison bars, while Mustard-Seed dances cheek-to-cheek with Puck in some thieves' hangout, humming to herself, "Thyme on my hands, you in my arms. . . ."

I really thought I had a winner in Norm, the delinquent Gnome. Original, dramatic, suitable for all age-groups. But I was wrong. He is useless to me, as I found out when I telephoned a publisher.

I telephoned the best publisher in London. I cannot, of course, mention his name but he was out so I spoke to his wife, Mrs Eyre Methuen.

"I've thought of this wonderful character for a book," I said. "He's a bent gnome called . . ."

That was as far as I got.

"A gnome?" she cried. "A *gnome?* You can't write books about a gnome! That's Enid Blyton's territory. You might be able to get away with writing about a gnome if you were another Enid Blyton, but that is what you will never be."

And so it has all been for nothing. I still have my beautiful little character, the crooked Norm, but I have to face facts:

"What's the good of a gnome if you're never Enid?"

Give your thoughts no tongue,
Nor any unproportion'd thought his act

William Shakespeare
'Hamlet'

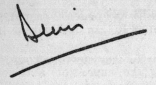

One of the many profound experiences which people without children are deprived of is that of sitting through a small daughter's Dancing Class Concert. I was conscripted for this numbness one long-ago Christmas when my daughter was six years old.

The reason she had joined the class in the first place was because she had somehow got herself mixed-up with a boy there. By mixed-up, I'm not implying she was mistaken for him, I mean there was an emotional involvement. It was a relationship I frowned upon, not merely because the lad bore a striking facial resemblance to Joan Crawford - after all, so does Mick Jagger - but because he was going on for at least twelve and I never believe there's any future in those May and December things. Also, and perhaps unreasonably, I had a sneaking feeling that any boy who voluntarily joins a Dancing Class cannot be all good.

However even at six, my daughter had, as they say, a whim of iron, so I took her along to meet the Principal. That lady's name was Signora Estrellita Mariposa which I didn't believe for a second, especially as her husband's name was Ornstein. She took against my child on sight. The moment we entered the room, "Much too tall!" was her opening comment. I immediately bristled, thinking she

215

was referring to me, but la Signora went on to aver that, for a member of a juvenile dancing troupe, the ideal specification is 'winsomely tiny'. Now while it is true that we are a lanky family and my daughter could have signed for the Harlem Globetrotters almost at birth, such a summary dismissal offended all my principles of equality in the arts. I therefore, argued the case powerfully, and after a certain amount of wallet-waving Signora Mariposa consented to allow her assistant to take the child into the next room for an audition.

"This one is a natural mover," announced that lady on their return, rather giving the impression that some six-year-olds had been found to be battery operated. With bad grace and at an exorbitant fee, the Principal agreed to take the child aboard.

The ensuing months I remember mainly for the nightly thumps on the ceiling as practice took place upstairs but the high point was reached in mid-November. "I'm going to be a Snowball!" exulted my daughter when she returned from class one cold evening. Some narrow-eyed questioning elicited the explanation that in the forthcoming annual concert - 'Santa Claus's Workshop!, A Seasonal Extravaganza of Song and Dance' - my daughter had won the coveted role over stiff opposition. "It's ninepence a ticket and everybody's got to come along and clap me," she ordered.

Everybody turned out to be me, all other blood-relations having had the foresight to develop Asian flu or go wintering in the Canary Isles. So, on that bleak December afternoon, I made my way to the concert's venue, the Cinema Café of the local Odeon.

All Cinema Cafés have a doomed air at the best of times, but on this occasion it was sheer Camus. And while we're on the literary references, you know that line of Sartre's about 'Hell is other people'? Well, it isn't. It's other people's *children*. There were sixty-seven pupils in that Dancing Class and every single one had a featured part in the two-and-a-half hour production. An unending parade of tidy winsomes, all of them bedaubed in lip-stick and greasepaint and red dots in the corners of their eyes, like a procession of depraved midgets.

I did notice, though, that the entrance of each one was greeted by loud localised plaudits from whichever area of the auditorium his or her family group was located. This showed me where my own duty lay. "When my child comes on," I vowed, "I will make up in vociferousness what I lack in numbers."

So when the orchestra - Miss Larby on piano and tambourine - struck up 'Winter Wonderland', I was ready. From the months of overhead thumping I knew this to be the tune to which we did our bit, so I took a deep breath. And when that glittering white Snowball tittuped on from behind the papier-mâché icicles, I rose to my feet and let out the full Sammy Davis Jnr whoop. "Wah-hoo! Yowee! Great, great! The kid's a sensation! Let's hear it for a really wonderful performer! Encore, encore! A-one more time!"

It was when the Snowball burst into terrified tears that I realised two elements were amiss. One, her physique was of an unfamiliar tinyness; two, there were twenty-three other Snowballs entering behind her.

I had, as was explained to me afterwards, whooped it up for the wrong Snowball. My daughter was number sixteen in the Snowball line. At the time though, the father of the hysterical Snowball spun round and punched me in the throat. I kicked him in the elbow (no, I can't think how), the police were called, I was ejected and Signora Mariposa summarily withdrew my daughter from the Concert, not even allowing her to stay and wave in the Finale. "I shall never permit a tall tot on stage again," she snarled.

Next day she expelled her from the class completely, claiming that the whole ugly incident would never have taken place had it not been for the child's excessive height. My daughter, for her part, blamed the whole thing on me and left home as soon as she reached adolescence. She is now in North Cornwall living with an unemployed rifle-range attendant who bears a striking facial resemblance to Linda Darnell.

I can only hope that the sorry tale offers a guide-line to any other fathers who may have small daughters about to appear in Dancing Class Concerts. Unless they are of the requisite tinyness - keep your mouth shut when they make their entrance. As Polonius advised Laertes:

"Give your tots no tongue,
For any unproportion'd tot is sacked."

Half a loaf is better than no bread

Proverb

Frank

Oh, believe me, it is not all glamour and laughter being Bimbo the Clown. Lots of you must have seen me when Potter and Ginsberg's Mammoth Imperial Circus visited your town. We usually pitched our big top in the car-park behind the pub.

I was the comic little chappie with baggy trousers and a ginger wig who ran on after the elephant. It was, from time to time, dangerous work.

Now no man is made of wood, not even Woden, The Wooden Man - he had a wooden leg but the rest of him was painted and grained to match it - and there came a time when I felt the urge to marry and settle down.

But who would marry Bimbo the Clown? What lady would be happy to say "That's my husband over there", pointing to a tiny, white-faced figure in enormous boots, with a red pin-pong ball nose, sitting in a bucket of whitewash? During most of my appearances I was deluged with whitewash. I had so much of it poured over me that my first thought when we arrived at a new town was to find a vet and get my distemper inoculation.

The first lady I approached with a view to courtship was Rumpo, the Fat Lady. Like many vast ladies she was a gentle, kindly person, always willing to help out when a lorry got stuck in the mud. One day the electricity in my caravan went off when I was in the middle of doing my ironing and Rumpo went down on all fours and turned the generator by hand. So I pressed my suit on her.

When I took her to Brighton on our day off everything seemed set fair. I had a little Mini at that time so I hired a van and away we went, as happy as two children let out of school. We even found a children's playground and played seesaw, Rumpo on one end and me and the van on the other. But tragedy struck later that night on the way home. I had stopped the van and helped Rumpo out of the back to give the springs a rest. As my arm went round part of her waist I suddenly blurted out my secret wish that I might one day make her Mrs Bimbo.

She burst into laughter. She howled with mirth that I could ever think she would marry a clown. As I worked the handle and jacked her up into the back of the van my heart was near breaking point.

Hath not a clown eyes? Hath not a clown hands, affections, passions? If you prick us, do not jets of water squirt out from our eyebrows? If you tickle us, doth not our ginger wig stand on end and the toes of our boots emit steam? If you poison us, doth not our bow-tie revolve?

Hurt and bruised, I scarcely spoke to another lady for some years. Then the side-show department of the circus acquired a new attraction, George-Ina, Half-Man Half-Woman. From delicate oval face to hairy legs, a vision of delight.

I was immediately attracted. There was a natural reticence there which appealed to me. Many circus-folk are over-friendly and are forever popping into your caravan but George-Ina, well - he kept himself to herself.

Perhaps the affair might have gone no further had not fate stepped in. One Sunday evening I returned late to the big top to hear screams and shouts. And George-Ina's unmistakable voice·

"HE-lp!"

A terrible scene greeted me as I rushed in. It seems that

Flexo, the Indiarubber Man, had been on one of his benders. He was clutching George-Ina to him and, inflamed with cheap liquor, was threatening that unless she agreed to spend the night in his caravan he would release the lion from its cage to claw all and sundry.

Everybody from the circus was there, and they all turned to me.

"Flexo," I said levelly. "You're twisted."

He merely snarled.

An icy calm came over me. Putting on my ping-pong nose to give myself confidence I moved unobtrusively to the side of Madam Zaza, the Human Cannonball, and said to her, very quietly:

"Madam Zaza, will you do me the pleasure of inserting yourself up your cannon, fusing yourself where necessary?"

She slipped away like a shadow.

Affecting nonchalance, I sauntered towards the cannon, muttering to the others as I passed, "Hide behind something in case Madam Zaza ricochets."

Once at the cannon I swiftly swung it until the muzzle pointed straight at the Indiarubber Man's heart.

"All right, Flexo!" I shouted, a new authority in my voice. "Drop George-Ina and walk slowly forwards with your hands above your head. Make one false move and I'll fill you full of Madam Zaza!"

He knew he was beaten. He unhanded George-Ina and stumbled forward. At that moment the local police arrived and took him away. The Indiarubber Man is now in Wormwood Scrubs prison, doing a stretch.

George-Ina fell into my waiting arms, and suddenly we were alone under the big top.

"Dear sir/madam," I whispered, "will you be mine?"

"I wish I could make up my mind," George-Ina whispered back. "Half of me wants to, but the other half is not so sure. . . ."

"Then let me make your mind up for you!" I cried, and picking her up in my arms I ran with her to the sideshow

221

marked See The Vicar Starving In A Barrel, where the vicar kindly interrupted his supper long enough to marry us.

People sometimes ask me whether I have not missed something, sharing my life with somebody who is half a gentleman and half a lady. Perhaps. But on a wintry evening, when we are snug in our caravan, me washing the whitewash out of my smalls, George-Ina varnishing her nails or lighting up her pipe, I think to myself - why cry for the moon when I have the stars?

Half a love is better than no bride.

'The Way To The Stars'

Title of Film

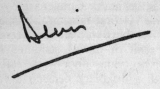

The most eloquent example of graffiti I can recall seeing was written on a road-sign. Under the notice 'Cul de Sac' someone had scrawled the words 'What isn't?'

Even if I had failed to recognise the handwriting, the sentiment would have identified the writer for me: Neville Pacefoot, the text-book example of what pop psychiatrists call 'a victim personality'. From early childhood, life treated him like the back wall of a squash court.

Neville's first brush with calamity came during his Boy Scout days. While he was helping an old lady across a street they both got run over. After a three-hour operation, he was taken off the danger-list and they allowed him to sit up and look at his Get Well cards. The first one was so amusing, he burst out laughing and broke eight stitches. Opening the next one he cut his finger and developed blood-poisoning.

Those were the earliest intimations that, in this super-market we call Existence, Neville had grabbed the shopping-cart with the wonky wheel. At the outbreak of War he persuaded the RAF to accept him, despite the fact that two of his toes had been crushed shapeless. (By a falling First Aid Cabinet.) He immediately became the only serviceman to get wounded during his Preliminary Medical

Examination. While the Medical Officer was sounding his chest, Neville noticed an Air Vice-Marshal entering the room, so he threw up a salute. It pulled the rubber tube of the stethoscope clean out of the M.O.'s head, and when the metal ear-pieces snapped back, that was the last of Neville's teeth. Nevertheless he persevered with the training and passed out as Sergeant Air Gunner.

The stripes did not survive his first mission. He spent that whole trip to and from Hamburg with his face pressed against the fuselage, the result of having slammed his handle-bar moustache in the plane door just before take-off. Invalided out with a disability pension a few months later, having been run over by an ambulance, he was directed to agricultural work and spent six months on a farm before a cow fell on him.

I lost touch with Neville for a while after the War, although I kept reading about him in such periodicals as the *Journal Of The Road Accident Research Centre,* whose cover he made four times. After he'd achieved national headlines as the first driver to break a leg by catching his foot in a car safety-belt, his insurance company wrote to ask for their calendar back. "It's like giving life cover to a lemming," the letter said.

It was around about this time that Neville's wife finally decided to leave him. For some time now she had found herself writing lipstick messages like "Enough's enough!" across the bedroom mirror, but when it was discovered that their daughter had been put in the family way by their son's Probation Officer, Mrs Pacefoot called it a day. She was given custody of the house, the furniture and the children, leaving Neville with only his savings, which had been safely invested in a pharmaceutical company making cyclamates.

From then on, things went steadily downhill. Fired from his job - his employer claimed that Neville's frequent trips to Intensive Care Units were inconsistent with being Manager of a Health Food Shop - he was obliged to seek whatever work he could. The day he was caught in the rain while carrying two thousand free samples of a new detergent, Neville gave way to despair and 'phoned the Samaritan organisation. The line was engaged.

How deeply his self-confidence had been shaken I did not realise till our next meeting. It took place as usual in a Casualty Ward, this time at St. Mary's, where he had been rushed after swallowing a fishbone.

"Well, that's not unique," I said consolingly. "That happens to lots of people."

"Not when they're eating a chocolate mousse."

I discounted the strain in his tone at first, putting it down to the fact that he was also awaiting trial on a serious charge. While driving along the Bayswater Road, he'd put his hand out to indicate a right turn. His signal coincided with the arrival alongside of a motor-cycle policeman who had accelerated up to Neville's window to congratulate him on his courteous driving. Neville's hand smashed him right in the mouth.

"You must try and look on the bright side," I said. "Worse things happen at sea."

"I've been at sea," he said. "I was the only person on board to get lockjaw and seasickness at the same time. Know what I'm beginning to think? I'm coming round to the conclusion that perhaps life isn't a cabaret, old chum."

I must admit to some feeling of uneasiness when I bade him farewell and, in the event, my forebodings were justified. Neville left the hospital with every intention of making his quittance of life. The notion of throwing himself in front of a train seemed a fitting response to a world which had placed so many hazards in his own path.

He made his way swiftly to King's Cross but just outside the station he was halted by someone tugging his sleeve. It was an old woman. "Spare a silver piece, kind sir," she said. "Only a small silver piece."

"What for?" he asked.

"A sprig of lucky white heather."

Despite the fact that fate had blunted most of Neville's physical features, his sense of irony remained keen. With a faint smile he handed her his last pound-note and thrust the sprig of heather into his button-hole. There was something to be relished in the idea of casting himself in the path of a fast express while wearing a good-luck token.

Making his way to the platform where the 3.35 to Carlisle stood, he stationed himself in front of the engine. When the guard blew his whistle, he closed his eyes tightly, waited to hear the first turn of the mighty wheels, then flung himself forward.

Philosophical profundities are not really my speed but I will venture to offer you a small one: when you're a loser - it's no use even expecting to win. The train went out backwards.

A lady porter picked Neville up off the line and dusted him down. As she was due to go off duty in a few minutes anyway, she took him home with her and have him a cup of tea, with some of her home-made ginger cake.

He's now living with her in quite blissful sin just outside Leatherhead, where they're running a small but thriving everything-shop.

Its name? Well, I suppose, in a wry kind of way, it's appropriate:

THE WHITE HEATHER STORES.

'Goodbye, Mr Chips'

James Hilton
Title of Novel

Frank

I am usually such a happy little chap, ever ready to dispel gloom with a merry quip or a saucy *bon mot*. I don't think that I would be breaking a confidence if I reveal that many years ago the lady with a mole who taught Sunday School at the Congregational Church referred to me as 'one of Nature's sunbeams'.

But a few months ago, I changed. Instead of dashing about the house wreathed in smiles and throwing off jolly epigrams I took to leaning silently against the wallpaper, scowling and plucking at the hem of my jacket.

The change came over me one day when I was lunching at the BBC canteen. I looked down at my tray, veal-loaf fritters and a waffle, and the awful realisation dawned that the meal epitomised my career; frittering my time away, and waffling on the radio. I had achieved nothing for which I would be remembered by posterity.

But what to do about it? What mark does one have to make so that when one is dead and gone one will be remembered long after one is forgotten?

The answer came to me on a bench in Hyde Park, where I was sitting brooding. A Japanese tourist beside me was fanning his face with a folded copy of the *Evening Standard* and a headline caught my eye; 'Paul Getty pays

£15,000 for National Gallery's "Washerwoman".' This seemed to me to be a stiff price to pay for recruiting domestic staff, even for a man reputedly not short of a bob, so my curiosity was aroused. I found that by getting on my knees in front of the man and synchronising my head with the oscillations of the newspaper I could read the whole piece. What emerged from the article was that Paul Getty had bought a terra-cotta portrait head from the National Gallery. It was a study by Rodin of his washerwoman, Mme Gautier. She was a friendly, excitable woman, aged thirty-four, with two daughters, etc. etc.

Of course! The way to go down to posterity is to be sculptured! If the biography of an unknown washerwoman could, a hundred years after her death, still cool the brow of a Japanese tourist, surely the same fame would attend me? I can see the newspaper article now - 'A terra-cotta head changed hands for £15,000,000 today. It is reputedly the head of F. Muir, who lived a hundred years ago. Now famous, he was little known at the time being by trade a fritterer and waffler. A lady with a mole once called him "One of Nature's sunbeams", and certainly his noble brow betokens . . .' etc.

I set to at once to sculpt a terra-cotta head of myself to present to the National Gallery.

It seemed to me that the best way to ensure a likeness would be to work from photographs. So I persuaded the Egham Photographic Society to help. Eighty of them turned up one sunny Saturday. I formed them into a circle, stood in the middle, 'click', and a week later I had eighty photographs of my head, each taken from a slightly different angle.

The next problem was the terra-cotta. I always thought the word referred to beefy nursemaids who hurled the baby into its cot, but it turned out to be reddish clay. Happily our house is on gravel soil so I only had to dig down some five feet before striking clay. It was somewhat yellow so I mixed it with a tin of dark-brown boot-polish.

I had about enough terra-cotta to make two heads, each

about the size of a grapefruit, so I decided to make a test run on one of the lumps first, just in case sculpting was more difficult than it looked.

I bashed the clay into shape with my fists and then pushed it about with a spoon and a toothpick until it began to look something like a human head. I was not attempting a likeness this time, which was a good thing because I had managed to get both ears on the same side. And three nostrils to the one nose.

Then into the oven it went, one hour at Regulo Mark 4.

When it came out - disaster. For some reason the whole head had slumped and spread. It still looked vaguely like a head but the head of a baboon.

"It's bound to sag when it's all in a lump," said my wife. "It's the same with pastry. What you want to do is treat it like we do a pie. Make it hollow, fill it with dried peas so that it keeps its shape, then lay the top on, pinching the edges together as you do with pastry."

Which is what I did. It was a tricky operation with a tacky lump of clay-and-boot-polish, and it took nearly a pound of dried peas to fill it, but I managed it. Then I lined up my eighty photographs, took spoon in hand, and started.

Who can explain the workings of fate? Was it a fluke? Was it the awakening of latent genius? All I can say for sure is that after ten minutes with spoon and toothpick I had produced a startling likeness of myself, an amazing little portrait head which the National or any other gallery would be proud to shove in a glass case next to the postcard counter in the foyer. I shouted for my wife to come and see it.

"Incredible!" she breathed. "So lifelike, and exact. And, sort of, peaceful!"

"So it should be," I replied. "It's full of peas." (I was quite my old self again.)

With infinite care we carried the head through to the kitchen and slid it into the cooker. As my wife closed the oven door I drew a chair up to the oven and prepared for a long vigil.

"No you don't!" said my wife. "There's nothing more you can do until the clay is baked. Let's go to the pictures."

It was a Saturday, and on Saturdays my son often dropped in. He had finished at university and was working in the City. Down a hole in the City, digging up Roman remains before office blocks cemented them away for ever. It was his practice to nip home sometime over the weekend with his pockets full of clothes to be washed, stand up in the bath and scrape Thames mud and medieval effluent off his salient features, eat whatever he could find in the house as long as it was hot and preferably smothered in chips, and disappear, leaving a laconic note on the kitchen table.

We arrived home from the pictures. I made straight for the oven. As I had my hand on the oven door I heard my wife saying, "Hello, Jamie's been home. Funny. I don't remember leaving out a -"

At that moment I opened the oven door to look at my masterpiece. And the oven was empty.

I knew instinctively what had happened, of course. "Farewell posterity," I whispered to myself as I held my hand out for Jamie's note.

Yes, there it was in black and white. Just five words:
"Good pie. Missed the chips".

Jilly Cooper
SUPER MEN AND SUPER WOMEN
Her brilliantly funny guide to the sexes

Whatever their grading, Super Man or Slob, Super Woman or Slut, Jilly submits them all to remorseless scrutiny. In public and private, home, office or bed, none escapes her beady eye - from guardsmen to gigolos, debs to divorcees, stockbrokers to sex fiends, tarts to Tory ladies.

W. C. Sellar   R. J. Yeatman
1066 AND ALL THAT

A book that has itself become part of our history. The authors made the claim that 'All the History you can remember is in the Book' - and for most of us, they were probably right. But it is their own unique interpretation of events that has made the book a classic; the result is an uproarious satire upon textbook history and our confused recollections of it.

thelwell.

TOP DOG
Thelwell's Complete Canine Compendium

As every experienced dog-owner knows, man's best friend is a complex bundle of appetites, instincts and winsome wiles. Few first-time pet-owners will realise, however, just what a responsibility they are taking on. So Thelwell has kindly provided them with this invaluable handbook full of advice on choosing, training, feeding, exercising and caring for our four-legged friends. It also emphasises the importance of protecting one's own interests - not to mention those of one's neighbours - for an ill-trained hound will soon develop a healthy disrespect for law and order. Here is a superb collection designed to give every dog-owner a new leash on life in the canine world.

PENELOPE

Penelope, that vociferous heroine of Thelwell's famous riding academy, has something to say on almost every aspect of the human condition, however hair-raising her own may be at the time. Ponies and philosophy go hand-in-hand when Penelope is around.

thelwell.

ANGELS ON HORSEBACK
- and elsewhere

Thelwell really understands the English countryside, its animals and people, and can appraise with sympathetic eye both horses and the horsey. That is why his drawings adorn the studies of some of the fiercest M.F.H.s in the country as well as being sure pin-up material in many Pony Club Members' dens.

The angels in *Angels on Horseback* are children, but there is plenty here about their parents. Both for those who know Thelwell, and for those who have not met him before, this book is a savoury at all time - but especially after attending a gymkhana.

THELWELL COUNTRY

Thelwell Country is the English countryside, only more so. His foxhunters and farmers, picnickers and gypsies, and his notoriously pony-struck children, are all representative of man in uneasy communion with nature.

The people and animals Thelwell laughs at are real: he knows the countryside intimately. Those who have delighted in Thelwell's cartoons will know what to expect. This is (with occasional excursions into country towns and even into Scotland) a hilarious initiation into the realities of rural England.